THE MOIRA PRESS
2010

PORPHYRY OF TYRE

PORPHYRY OF TYRE

AN INTRODUCTION TO THE *TETRABIBLOS* OF PTOLEMY

EDITED AND TRANSLATED BY
ANDREA L. GEHRZ

THE MOIRA PRESS
Portland, Oregon

The Moira Press

Portland, Oregon

All rights reserved
Copyright © 2010 by Moira Press
Cover design by Scott Gerke

Published by Moira Press
www.moirapress.org

All rights reserved. No part of this publication may be reproduced in any form without permission of the author, except for the inclusion of brief quotations.

ISBN 978-0-9827893-0-8

Acknowledgements

I have received much support and many favors along the path to publishing this translation. First and foremost, I would like to thank Scott, Angelene, and the entirety of my friends, who have been my personal cheerleaders throughout this long and arduous process. I would also like to thank the professors at Kepler College for introducing me to hellenistic astrology and the need for translations of the hellenistic texts. Also, I must specifically acknowledge Kenneth D. Miller, for his genuine and unending assistance with everything from scans to book references to editing. Beyond that, I could not have even begun to create this translation without the knowledge and aid of Chris Brennan, the person who initially presented the text to me, and with whom I spent hours discussing the history of astrology, Greek technical jargon, and translation in general. I am also indebted to my dear friend, Judith Hill, for her help with publication details and her encouragement to make this text available to the public. I would like also to express my deepest gratitude to Ed Alletto, with whom I spent hours discussing the manner in which to apply real time interpreting theory to a written translation. And lastly, I cannot fail to mention the person who guided me to this point linguistically, my exacting and masterful Greek teacher, Laurie Cosgriff.

Table of Contents

INTRODUCTION TO THE TEXT I
INTRODUCTION TO GREEK AND PTOLEMAIC COSMOLOGY VI
INTRODUCTION TO ASPECTS AND BEAMS X
TRANSLATOR'S INTRODUCTION XII

1. "Introduction" 1
2. "The Things Signified by the Revolutions of the Sun, Moon, and the remaining Planets" 2
3. "The Places in Which the Planets Reach Apogee and Perigee" 8
4. "Nocturnal and Diurnal Planets" 10
5. "The Naming of Certain Zones and Signs to the Specific Planets" 11
6. "Exaltation" 12
7. "Co-rulers of the Places" 13
8. "Testimony" 14
9. "Right-handed and Left-handed Aspects" 15
10. "Transmission" 15
11. "Planets in Union or Closing In on One Another" 16
12. "Separating" 16
13. "More on Separating" 17
14. "Being Surrounded" 17
15. "Being Enclosed" 18
16. "Intervention" 18
17. "Transference" 19

18.	"Collection"	19
19.	"Turning Away"	20
20.	"Upon the Tenth"	20
21.	"Superiority"	21
22.	"Juxtaposition"	22
23.	"Void of Course"	22
24.	"The Casting of Rays"	23
25.	"Chariots"	25
26.	"Cooperation"	25
27.	"Counteraction"	26
28.	"Maltreatment"	26
29.	"Keeping Guard"	27
30.	"The Sign Ruler, the Lord, and The Ultimate Ruler of the Nativity"	29
31.	"Signs of Correspondence"	32
32.	"Signs of Equal Power"	32
33.	"Signs that are Visible to One Another and the Magnitude of the Day"	33
34.	"Unconnected Signs"	34
35.	"Cadent Houses"	34
36.	"Productive Signs"	35
37.	"The Conception Sign of the Sun"	35
38.	"The Conception Sign of the Moon"	36
39.	" The Twelfth Part"	37
40.	"Masculine and Feminine Signs"	38
41.	"The Ascensional Times of the Signs"	39
42.	"The Amount of Time Equivalent to Each Degree of Each Ascending Sign"	43
43.	"A Method for Distinguishing the Boundaries, by Degree, Between the Angular, Cadent and Succedent Houses"	45
44.	"The Parts of the Body Signified by Each Sign"	47
45.	"The Parts of the Body Ruled by Each of the Planets"	48
46.	"The Clothing, Dyes and Colors Ruled by Each Planet"	51
47.	"The Thirty-Six Decans and The Paranatellonta	

	AND THEIR ASSOCIATED CHARACTERISTICS"	51
48.	"THE FIXED STARS AND THE POWER OF THE PARANATELLONTA"	53
49.	"THE BOUNDS ACCORDING TO THE EGYPTIANS, AND PTOLEMY AND THE DARK DEGREES"	54
50.	"THE ASSIGNING OF THE PARTS OF THE BODY TO THE SIGNS"	55
51.	"AN OUTLINE OF THE DIFFERENT METHODS FOR CALCULATING TRINES, SQUARES, SEXTILES, AND OPPOSITIONS"	56
52.	"THE TIMES OF LIFE IN REGARDS TO THE ANGULAR, CADENT AND SUCCEDENT HOUSES"	59
53	"THE MANNERS THROUGH WHICH THE INDICATIONS OF THE PLANETS COME TO FRUITION"	61
54.	"A CONSIDERATION REGARDING THE TESTIMONY OF THE PLANETS"	63
55.	"THE BEAMS OF THE PLANETS"	64

APPENDIX OF SCHOLIA BY DEMOPHILUS (OR THEOPHILUS)	66
SECTION 2	67
SECTION 30	68
SECTION 42	69
SECTION 53	70
WORKS CITED	72

Introduction to the Text

The *Introduction to the Tetrabiblos of Ptolemy* is actually a compilation of ideas from a number of "ancient" astrological authors, written by an author who would also be considered "ancient" to the modern reader. While there has been much debate over the true authorship of this text, it has been generally attributed to the philosopher Porphyry of Tyre. Regardless of who actually wrote this *Introduction*, it is an important text in the context of the history of astrology, in that it seems to have been written in an attempt to clarify certain astrological concepts that still remained unclear at the time. As the title suggests, the *Introduction to the Tetrabiblos* was intended to accompany and clarify the *Tetrabiblos* of Claudius Ptolemy (c.100-175 C.E.)[1]. Ptolemy wrote two important texts pertaining to the history of astrology, the *Tetrabiblos* and the *Almagest*. While the *Almagest* focused solely on the mathematics of astronomy, the *Tetrabiblos* focused on astrology. In the *Tetrabiblos*, Ptolemy addressed a variety of topics, including nocturnal and diurnal charts, aspects, conception charts, and even a method with which one could calculate the native's length of life. The *Tetrabiblos* is quite extensive and at times hard to understand. Thus, Porphyry compiled this text in order to clarify the concepts presented in

---

[1] Claudius Ptolemy. *The Almagest*. translated by G. J. Toomer (New Jersey: Princeton University Press, 1998), 1.

the *Tetrabiblos* by using the words of other astrologers before his time, including Antiochus of Athens, Thrasyllus, Timaeus, Petosiris, Apollinarus, and of course, Ptolemy.

Porphyry himself was a Neoplatonic philosopher who lived somewhere between the years of 234-305 C.E. Approximately sixty works have been attributed to him, on subjects ranging from religion to philosophy to musical theory to astrology. Some of his titles include the *Life of Pythagoras, On Abstinence from Eating Food from Animals, the Life of Plotinus,* and *On the Cave of the Nymphs*[2]. Astrology was only one of the many subjects about which Porphyry wrote.

The specific source text I have used for this translation is a critical edition of Porphyry's *Introduction to the Tetrabiblos* which was compiled, edited, and published in 1940 by German scholars Emilie Boer and Stephen Weinstock. The manuscript itself can be found in Book Five, Part Four of the *Catalogus Codicum Astrologorum Graecorum* (pp187-228), an extensive collection of ancient Greek astrological texts. Emilie Boer was a student of Franz Boll (1867-1924), a German scholar who extensively studied Ptolemy's works, as well as biographical information about Ptolemy's life. When Boll died in 1924, Boer carried on his work, and eventually published the critical edition which has been used for the translation.

In their Latin introduction to this text, Boer and Weinstock bring up the objection by historians that Porphyry was not the true author. The objections they address seem to have been derived from the fact that Porphyry was a Neoplatonic philosopher and a disciple of Plotinus, with whom he lived and studied for six years. Neoplatonists in general, and Plotinus included, did indeed have some objections to astrology. In his

---

[2] Eyjólfur Emilsson, "Porphyry", *The Stanford Encyclopedia of Philosophy (Fall 2009 Edition)*, Edward N. Zalta (ed.), URL = <http://plato.stanford.edu/archives/fall2009/entries/porphyry/>

translation of *Plotinus*, A. H. Armstrong notes that Plotinus didn't necessarily admonish astrology altogether, but instead had specific objections to the manner in which astrologers observed the planets in respect to earthly life. Plotinus believed that astrologers exaggerated the affects of the planets, that they separated the influence of the planets from the totality of the universe, and he also found some of their techniques to be unscientific[3]. It is because of these objections by his teacher Plotinus, and Neoplatonists in general, that Porphyry originally had been doubted by historians as the true author of this text.

Since the year that this text was published, there has been further discussion about who wrote it, and some historians propose that different sections should be attributed to different authors. In his article "From Alexandria to Baghdad to Byzantium: The Transmission of Astrology", David Pingree argues that Porphyry was indeed the true author of sections 1-45, which also show a remarkable parallel to Antiochus of Athens, an author from which Porphyry seems to have derived much of his information[4]. In general, Porphyry's *Introduction to the Tetrabiblos* is thought to be one of three existing commentaries on the *Tetrabiblos*, along with a commentary by a Neoplatonic philosopher named Proclus (412-485 C.E.), and also the notes (scholia) that had been added to the Porphyry text by an editor named Demophilus[5]. Demophilus was a later astrologer who lived and wrote in Constantinople around 990 C.E.[6]. There are indeed scholia that appear in the footnotes of the critical edition, which have been translated here and included as an appendix,

---

[3] Plotinus. *Plotinus,* vol. 2, translated by A. H. Armstrong (Cambridge: Harvard University Press, 1966) 55.

[4] David Pingree, "From Alexandria to Baghdad to Byzantium. The Transmission of Astrology," *International Journal of the Classical Tradition* 8, no. 1 (2001): 7.

[5] Claudius Ptolemy. *The Tetrabiblos,* translated by F.E. Robbins (Cambridge: Harvard University Press, 1940) xvi.

[6] Pingree 8

with the references in the body of text appearing as capital letters in parenthesis. Pingree suggests that sections 47-52 of Porphyry were also most likely additions made by Demophilus.

Boer and Weinstock mention that they were unsure as to whether or not the scholia were actually written by Demophilus, or perhaps by an earlier author, Theophilus. According to Pingree, Theophilus was an author and translator who was born in Edessa around 695 C.E[7]. The main concept to understand here, is that the true author or authors of this text are entirely unclear. Most likely, Porphyry was the true author of a large portion of this text, but not the entirety of the text, and exactly who wrote the other portions has not yet been clarified. One last thing to mention is that sections 46 and 53-55 are stylistically different than all other sections, and thus, these also might have been commentary added by a later author. Pingree also argues that these sections should not be attributed to Porphyry[8].

In that my approach to this text has been that of a translator and not a historian, I will not attempt to clarify any questions of authorship here. I have, however, found it necessary and useful to include these questions, in that they inform the reader about the historical context of the text that is being read. And for the sake of clarity, I will consistently refer to "Porphyry" when discussing the author of the text below, with the understanding that different sections may indeed have been written by various authors.

By virtue of the fact that Porphyry has written a compilation here, there are a variety of verb tenses that appear in the text, which in English, translate to a range of different pronouns. Many of the short sections use the third person singular verb form, which would literally translate to "he said" or "he says". I assume that Porphyry is meaning either Ptolemy or Antiochus in

---

[7] Pingree 13
[8] Pingree 8

these sections, but it is not at all clear to whom Porphyry is referring. In other sections, the third person plural verb form is used, which translates as "they said" or "they say", and still it is unclear to whom this "they" is referring. My general approach has been to make this text readable, and thus I have aimed for fluency in these situations by using natural English constructions such as passive voice or a more general voice. I do, however, feel it necessary to make mention of these variations for the reader who might have a knowledge of Greek language or history, and might want to inquire further into such intricate matters. Moreover, there are places in which the first person singular and plural verb forms have been used, and in these places I have have found it pertinent to preserve the original forms, and thus have translated these sentences with the pronouns "I" or "we". In these parts of the text, I have assumed that Porphyry (or another author) is making his own additional commentary, which is why I have felt it essential to maintain the integrity of the verbs in such places.

I should also make mention of the fact that, in the Greek text, there is no variation in typography, meaning that the text within almost every section is essentially composed of one long paragraph. I have made divisions between paragraphs here in an attempt to make the text readable, but by no means is this construction mimicking the actual format of the critical edition.

Lastly, I have made a stylistic decision to include the Greek headings in the body of the text, alongside the English translations of these headings. Accordingly, I have also italicized the English words that are representative of the Greek concepts being illustrated in each section, in order that the reader can compare the Greek words in the headings with the italicized English words in each section. In this way, the reader can compare the terms and engage in a deeper layer of understanding of the Greek source text.

Introduction to Greek and Ptolemaic Cosmology

When trying to understand hellenistic astrology, it is very important to also understand how the Greek astronomers and astrologers understood the cosmos as a whole. This information is crucial in comprehending the manner in which the ancient astrologers constructed an astrological chart. I will not delve into all of the intricacies of the Greek cosmology here, such as epicycles and exact calculations, but instead, will attempt to provide an explanation that is pertinent specifically to astrology. For more information on these specific topics, the reader may want to consult the *Almagest* specifically, or a book such as Michael J. Crowe's *Theories of the World: From Antiquity to the Copernican Revolution*[9].

As is illustrated in the *Almagest*, Ptolemy's extensive work on astronomy, the ancient Greeks perceived the heavens as being spherical in shape, with the unmoving earth situated in the center of this sphere. This sphere was thought to revolve around the earth, rising up in the east and setting in the west once each day, and the planets were thought to rise up on the eastern horizon

---

[9] Michael J. Crowe, *Theories of the World: From Antiquity to the Copernican Revolution* (Mineola: Dover Publications, 2001).

and set in the west along this sphere during its daily revolution around the earth. Ptolemy also described a planetary motion that countered the motion of this spherical rising and setting. As he described in Book I, Section 8 of the *Almagest*, "There are two different primary motions in the heavens. One of them is that which carries everything from east to west: it rotates them with an unchanging and uniform motion along circles parallel to each other...The other motion is that by which the spheres of the stars perform movements in the opposite sense to the first motion[10]." This second motion that Ptolemy mentions is the opposite motion along which the planets travel through the zodiac and increase in zodiacal longitude, the sun moving one degree a day, the moon traveling thirteen degrees, mercury moving approximately one degree, etc.

This Greek image of the cosmos, then, matches directly with the image that an astrologer sees when he or she looks at an astrological chart. The circle of the zodiac is representing the circular shape of the sphere that was thought to rise and set around the earth. And thus, the construction of the basic template of an astrological chart, including the Ascendant, Descendant, Midheaven, Nadir, and the houses, is derived specifically from this idea of the first motion of the heavenly sphere. Ptolemy even mentions in the *Almagest* that six zodiacal signs were thought to be visible above the horizon at any given time, while six signs were thought to be hidden under the horizon[11]. This accounts for the Ascendant-Descendant axis line that splits a nativity in half. If the modern reader can thus imagine the chart as it was thought to represent this heavenly sphere, then the manner in which the hellenistic astrologers constructed a chart becomes entirely clear.

A perfect example of the Greek astrological way of explaining a nativity in respect to the first motion of the cosmos can be seen in

---

[10] Toomer 45-46.
[11] Toomer 42.

section 30, at the end of paragraph 6, when Porphyry writes the phrase "τὸν ἐπαναφερόμενον τῷ μεσουρανήματι". This phrase literally means to "rise up after the Midheaven", and in reference to an astrological chart, this describes a planet in the eleventh house. In order to think like a Greek astrologer, then, the reader must imagine this first movement of the sphere of the heavens rising up in the east, carrying along with it the Midheaven, (or in this case the whole tenth house), and as it rides up on this celestial sphere, a planet rising up after it. This would then put a planet that is "rising up after the Midheaven" in the eleventh house of the astrological chart. Another example of this motion of the celestial sphere can be seen in the same section by use of phrases such as planets being "in the east" (ἐν τῷ ἀπηλιώτῃ) or "declining in the west" (ἀποκλινῃ ἐπὶ λίβα). These examples are specifically referring to planets being stronger when they are near the point of ascending above the horizon, and being weaker when they are nearer to setting under the horizon.

There are also references in hellenistic astrology to the second and opposing motion in the heavens. This motion is often mentioned by use of Greek terms for a planet that is "preceding" (ὁ προηγούμενος) and a planet that is "following" (ὁ ἑπόμενος). In the modern astrological chart, this would refer to planets that are ahead or behind one another in terms of zodiacal longitude. These terms are specifically describing the degrees along the zodiac "from which" and "to which" the planets are traveling.
An example of this can be found in Section 24 on the "casting of rays". Porphyry writes, "The leading planet in an aspect *casts a ray* onto the planet behind it. For example, a planet in Aries *casts a ray* by square to a planet in Capricorn, and by trine onto a planet in Sagittarius". It can be seen here, that the "leading planet" is leading in terms of zodiacal longitude. In terms of the planets moving through the zodiac, it is further along in its cycle than the planet in back.

It can be seen that the Greek astronomers and astrologers imagined the heavens in a manner very different from the modern astrologer, and thus, it is very useful to have an understanding of the astronomical worldview from which the modern chart has been derived. When the modern astrologer looks at an astrological chart, the chart itself does not appear to match the modern heliocentric understanding of the heavens; it does however replicate the ancient Greek view of the cosmos. And in this way, a glimpse into history proves very enlightening to the modern practitioner of the astrological arts.

Introduction to Aspects and Beams

It is also necessary to understand the manner in which the ancient astrologers understood and described aspects. In hellenistic astrology, planets were said to "cast rays" onto one another, which essentially meant that they were thought to send out planetary beams into the cosmos, which may or may not happen upon another planet. Porphyry first illustrates this idea at the end of Section 9 in his description of "right-handed and left-handed aspects". He mentions that there are "seven beams released by each of the planets; three that face upwards or north, three that go downwards or south, and one that shines exactly across to the opposite point".

This hellenistic planetary beam theory also is pertinent in Section 16 on "intervention," the section in which Porphyry suggests that planetary rays can be thrown between other planets, which in turn affects the outcomes of these planets. An understanding of planetary ray theory may also be useful in thinking about concepts such as aspects making an "equal-sided" line, an idea which is present in Section 10, on "transmission". If the planets were thought to send out beams into the cosmos, and an aspect were to become exact, then this beam could also be thought to create a geometric "line" in the cosmos.

Ancient Greek optical theory is also of interest in that Porphyry and other hellenistic astrologers often used visual references for planetary phenomenon. Planets were often said to "behold" one another, while certain signs were said to be able to "see" one another. A good example of this can be seen in Section 24 on the "casting of rays". In this section, Porphyry compares the idea that some planets "cast rays" while other planets merely "look upon" one another. In fact, Porphyry even suggests the idea that planets that "casts rays" are destructive while planets that "look upon" one another are not. Further research into this topic seems to explain why hellenistic astrologers so often used vision as a metaphor in their descriptions of astrological concepts, especially in terms of aspects. In ancient Greece, it was a common idea that visual perception occurred on account of a "visual beam" that extended out from the eye of the "beholder", onto the object being perceived. And in this manner, vision worked quite nicely as a comparison in terms of aspects or beams.

This common theory that vision occurred on account of beams being sent out by the eyes has been termed the "extromissive" theory of vision. Both Euclid and Plato were convinced of this theory, as was Ptolemy. According to Mark Smith in *Ptolemy's Theory of Visual Perception: an English Translation of the Optics*, the extromissionists believed that "vision [was] due to a sort of internal fire or flux that issued from the eye to strike an external object. Once touched by the outgoing flux, those objects [were] visually perceived, so, in a sense, the eye [saw] the physical world by shedding its own light upon it.[12]" As can be seen in this quote, both the eyes and the planets were thought to send out beams, and it is most likely for this reason that visual metaphors quite often appeared in hellenistic astrology.

---

[12] Mark A. Smith, *Ptolemy's Theory of Visual Perception: An English Translation of the "Optics" with Introduction and Commentary*, (Transactions of the American Philosophical Society: Volume 86, Part 2. Philadelphia: The American Philosophical Society, 1996) 22.

Translator's Introduction

My goal as a translator has been to make this ancient text accessible to the modern astrologer, who might find the history of astrology to be somehow enlightening. I do not present this as a modern technical text, but instead, as a readable version of an ancient text, inasmuch as it represents the history of our field. I have worked as a professional sign language interpreter for ten years, and thus my background and experience are in the field of language and translation, meaning that I have approached this text expressly from a linguistic standpoint. There are many historical questions surrounding this text, and while I have mentioned these inquiries in the preceding "Introduction to the Text", I have done so explicitly with the purpose of helping the reader understand the context of the text that has been translated. I have happily left the job of understanding the exact historical details to those with an expertise in the history of astrology. My utmost goal has been for the reader to be able to enjoy a fluent and readable translation, thus providing access to the hellenistic concepts as they were presented in the original language and culture of the hellenistic astrologers.

With that in mind, it must be said that as a translator, it is often challenging to convey exactly the concepts and the meaning intended by an original author, in that certain ideas are not similarly expressed in both the source language and the target language. For instance, when translating for a Deaf person, it is challenging to translate concepts relating to sounds or tones, because the Deaf consumer may not have access to such concepts. This is true for every culture across history and time, in that each culture has a unique worldview, and thus, has specific language surrounding that perception of the world. On account of the fact that most readers of a translated text do not inherently have access to the language of the source text, it could be argued that, without extra information, the reader can not truly access the mind of the original author. And in this respect, I have provided additional explanations of the Greek cosmology and aspect theory in order that the reader can fully grasp the meaning of the translation.

My philosophy on the role of a translator has also been derived from my many years in the field, and from having the rare opportunity to consistently practice translation in real time. It is my wholehearted belief that the role of a translator is not to alter a text or to fix mistakes in the text, but instead, to provide a pure and unaltered, yet conceptually accurate version of what is written in the source language. In regards to the translation that follows, there are certain parts of the source text that are troublesome, in that they are overly fragmented, lacking in sufficient context, or marred by grammatical errors. Consistent with my understanding of the role of a translator, I have left these inconsistencies in the body of the text, but have noted my concerns in the footnotes, in order that the reader who knows Greek can inquire further.

Above and beyond anything else, I truly hope that you enjoy reading this translation.

PORPHYRY OF TYRE

AN INTRODUCTION TO THE *TETRABIBLOS* OF PTOLEMY

Section 1 "Introduction"
Προοίμιον

Ptolemy, having had a thorough understanding of the heavenly bodies, and having himself observed the possible earthly outcomes that could be derived from a synthesized viewing of such bodies, took it upon himself to articulate clearly certain concepts that had been covered up and obscured by the ancients. In creating this specific text, I have thought it necessary to be very clear by first describing the basic concepts laid out in Ptolemy's works. I have also, in certain parts of this text, provided further explanation beyond that which has been laid out by Ptolemy, in order to clarify certain concepts and to elucidate all of the ideas that have gushed forth through his writing. For it seems best to convey these ideas in an applicable manner.

While Ptolemy was aware of many of the basic concepts laid out in this book, including *testimony*, *keeping guard*, *superiority*, and *the ultimate ruler of the chart*[13], he did not disclose exact examples of these

---

[13] See sections 8, 29, 21, and 30, respectively

concepts, which might raise doubts in regard to these ancient methods that were initiated well before our time. And so we have set out to convey these teachings, bound to us by the ancients, in a manner that is both concise yet well-arranged into separate sections, so that the concepts can be easily absorbed by the student who has yet to be initiated into these subjects.

Section 2

"The Things Signified by the Revolutions of the Sun, Moon and the Remaining Planets"

Περὶ τῶν ἀπὸ τοῦ Ἡλίου καὶ τῆς Σελήνης καὶ τῶν ἀστέρων ἐν ταῖς παρόδοις γινομένων ἐπισημασιῶν[14]

Just as a person might be the mightiest of all kings, the sun is the mightiest of all the heavenly bodies. The sun has been assigned to all things associated with the air and the earth, and it clearly defines and arranges such things, bringing them into some kind of order. The less mighty planets combine their energies with the sun, at times cooperating with the sun, and at other times thwarting his efforts. The four seasons of spring, summer, fall and winter are produced by the slanting of the ecliptic, and together the planets ultimately produce the heat and the cold present in each season, and are entirely responsible for the wind.

Through its unceasing energy, the sun appears to bring order and life to an otherwise disordered and lifeless world. It regulates the sperm and ovum that underlie the creation of all life. Its solar rays warm the ground and the seeds of life that swim in the waters, and it is able to mold and shape such things as its cosmic and life-giving rays pass over everything during its yearly circle through the cosmos. The sun works dutifully to turn the seeds that are ready,

---

[14] Robbins 5-19. This section seems to be a direct reference to Book I, Section 2 of the *Tetrabiblos*.

lying dormant in the earth, into sprouts and then later into plants. Yet simultaneously, the sun also arranges its affairs according to its own timing, having no sympathy for the fields that have been tilled, or the ships out at sea, or all the influences required to help plants and animals thrive.

And so it is necessary to closely observe the conditions of the planets and the fixed stars near to them, so that one might keep the fields and the ships and the plants safe and secure. This is not unlike the way in which animals prepare themselves for the winter by finding a calm place to lie motionless and warm, awaiting the chance to move to another more bountiful location when the weather warms, a place providing sweet smells and plenty of water. And the plants do the same as the animals, matching their cycle to that of the solar rays. They lie in the earth waiting for the right time, during which they sprout up in rows, eventually morphing into pleasant and beautiful blooming flowers. The completion of this cycle occurs when the plants bear their bountiful gifts, producing all varieties of fruits and vegetables.

The moon is the nearest to earth of all the planets and as she makes angles to these planets, she mingles her active forces with them, and filters the forces of the heavenly bodies through her beams and mixes them with the forces of the sun. And thus, the moon can be likened to the queen of the cosmos, being only secondary to the sun. She helps him to bring order to the world by defining the seasons, and especially the four weeks of each month. As the sun traverses around the entire zodiac in the course of a year, the moon simultaneously gathers the light from the sun and carries it from each new moon to the next, taking approximately 29.5 days to make one lunar cycle. This cycle mimics the four turning points of the solar year. From the rising phase until the first quarter phase in the spring, and onto the full moon phase in the summer, and then to the second quarter phase in the fall, and back to the phase of concealment in the winter (A)[15].

All affairs in life do not follow this exact cycle, but often things do come to pass in a very similar manner to the cycle between the sun and the moon. For many things ripen, wax, and wane along with this cycle. For instance, this can be seen in sea life, such as crabs, lobsters, sea urchins, and other hard-shelled animals such as these, which quite clearly get larger and smaller along with the moon. Even plants, when given some water and a little heat, will fatten their seeds and ripen their fruits, but everything existing underneath this process occurs on account of the moon walking through her phases. This cycle can also be seen as the moon watches over the monthly purification ritual of the menses in women. Even the rivers, streams and canals fill up and empty along with the waxing and waning of the moon; it is as if these cycles are a divine ritual, being arranged from high up above.

The sun and the moon create seven different phases together. The first phase occurs when the moon has arrived at a point 60 degrees from the sun, and appears to be crescent-shaped in the sky. The moon appears to be cut in half as she reaches 90 degrees from the sun, and at 120 degrees, she appears to be convex on both sides. The moon resembles a full orb when the sun and moon are 180 degrees apart, and at this point, her phases begin to decrease. When she reaches the point in which the sun precedes her by 120 degrees, she again appears convex on both sides, and at 90 degrees, she is again divided equally in half. At the 60 degree point, she again appears to be crescent-shaped in the night sky. And having made all of these configurations, the moon is carried by the rays of the sun into the phase which is called "the conjunction", and this moment indicates the conditions of the surrounding air and the atmosphere. The moon carries all of the significations of the

---

[15] (A) This notation, and all letters in parenthesis hereafter, refer to the scholia of Demophilus, which I have included in an appendix.

heavenly bodies and changes of weather to the sun, just as she in turn carries them to each of the planets.

Having provided this explanation, it is now necessary to give a complete account of the planetary risings as well as the particular synthesis that occurs when these same planets rise up alongside certain fixed stars. In general, it is important to know the significations of the eastern risings of the planets, the planetary stations, the solstices, the equinoxes, and above all, the solar and lunar eclipses. This information is significant because the things that are happening in the heavens at the moment of birth shall determine the planetary configuration in a nativity, and it is from this that we can interpret a chart in order to discover the most productive and sympathetic affinities of the planets by the nature of their signs. We can also examine the significations of the signs in which the planets are placed and the angular configurations that they make to one another. From this knowledge, a prognosis is born at the moment of a birth, foretelling the things that will happen to a person, both good things and bad things, which can be seen by the qualities of the planets, the ways in which the stars interact with one another, and by a thorough examination and synthesis of the many particular parts of a nativity.

Generally, the planets can be seen rising in the eastern part of the sky, presuming they do not fall within the area that is approximately fifteen degrees to either side of an exact conjunction to the sun. More specifically, Saturn, Jupiter, and Mars will be visible in the sky as they rise in the east, roughly 120 degrees distant from the sun, at which point these planets will make their first station, preparing to retrace their path. At this point, they will continue to move backwards as the sun travels through the sixth sign from them and eventually reaches an opposition to them. Throughout this time period when they are exactly opposite to the sun, the heavenly bodies will appear to rise in the sky at the beginning of the night, at the time of the sun's setting. From this point, the planets continue to move backwards until they approach another trine to the sun, at which point they will make their second station, and then finally are released and begin to advance forward.

In that, at this point, Saturn, Jupiter, or Mars are no longer moving retrograde but are now moving forward, they continue to advance into the section of degrees that rise after the sun, and continue to set in the evening until the sun reaches a conjunction with them. A planet is considered to be exactly conjunct with the sun when it is no farther than 59 minutes from the exact degree of the sun.

The fiery planet of Mars makes two unique angular configurations with the sun, which the authors who pay attention to such matters have noted to be a consistent deviation when compared to the other planetary cycles[16]. Mars makes its first peculiar movement by slowing down at its first stopping when it is rising in the east preceding the sun by merely 82 to 90 degrees. It completes its unusual cycle when it is rising after the sun at the same interval of 82 to 90 degrees, during which time it makes an evening setting. As has been mentioned above, each of the planets completes its cycle when it arrives at an exact conjunction with the sun, within less than one degree.

Venus and Mercury govern different human affairs on earth because of their close proximity to the sun, meaning that they both complete a running in more or less one day's time[17]. Because they

---

[16] Owen Gingerich, *The Eye of Heaven: Ptolemy, Copernicus, Kepler* (New York: American Institute of Physics, 1993) 9. Gingerich mentions that Ptolemy's calculations of the planet Mars showed irregularities that challenged the existing Greek cosmology. One of these observations is that Mars seemed to move forty percent faster on one half of its orbit than the other half. And secondly, the retrograde movement of Mars was irregular from one cycle to the next.

[17] This is most likely referring to the fact that, because Mercury and Venus both have a "bounded elongation" to the sun, meaning that they both only travel a certain distance away from the sun, they both complete one cycle around "the earth" in the span of one year. This means, then, that

are always close to the sun, Venus and Mercury appear in two different phases to the sun, the first phase occurring when they are approximately 15 degrees away from the sun on either side, meaning that they will be seen as a morning star, appearing in the heavens around the time of sunrise (B). The second phase occurs when these planets set in the evening, meaning that they are preceding or following the sun at an interval of greater than 15 degrees. When Mercury or Venus is situated more than 15 degrees away from the sun, and is also rising before the sun, it will set before the sun goes down, and will not be visible at night. When these two planets are 15 degrees away from the sun, but rise after the sun, they will make an evening setting, meaning that they will be visible in the night sky.

Venus makes its first station at around 47 degrees from the sun, while Mercury stops around 23 degrees away from the sun. After these planets make their first stations, they begin to move backwards in a retrograde motion, and after the second station, they go direct and move forward.

And it is necessary, in general, to understand that the stars as a whole always migrate into the degrees following them[18]. The appearance that the planets are always at the same degree is a deception that happens as a result of the manner through which the stars are seen with the eyes. In addition, one must consider the fixed stars, as Ptolemy has observed, for they become co-rulers to the planets by combining their natures with the planets and thus changing the nature of these planets. And on account of their blending natures with the wandering planets, they become co-rulers of the nativity, according to the descriptions, attributes, and unique features of the different regions.

---

they also move approximately one degree each day. For more information on this topic, refer to Crowe's *Theories of the World*, page 15.

[18] This is probably a direct reference to the "precession of the equinoxes". For a further discussion of this topic, see Crowe pages 8 and 9.

Section 3
"The Places in Which the Planets Reach Apogee and Perigee"
Περὶ ὧν Σ ἀστέρες ἐν τῷ βάθει ποιοῦνται ἀπογείων καὶ περιγείων σχηματισμῶν

It is essential to understand the four phases of the planets as they travel through the comsos, and how these configurations might affect the possible outcomes of the planets. The first configuration occurs when a planet is traveling down from its farthest point away from the earth into the middle portion of its orbit, and is thus moving from a place farther out on its loop to a place that is closer to the earth[19]. The second phase occurs when a planet is moving from this mid-section of its orbit to the part of its path that is closest to the earth, which is called its *perigee*. The third phase is when the planet is very close to the earth, but is leaving its point of *perigee*, and is thus moving to a higher up place as it moves away from the earth. The last part of a planet's orbit occurs when the planet has passed the middle part of its path, and is approaching the place in which it is farthest from the earth, its *apogee*.

It is important to be familiar with this cycle because planets that are moving away from their position of *apogee*, and approaching a conjunction with the sun, are moving forward. But as the planets continue to move away from this point of *apogee* and past the middle part of their orbit, they approach their first station at the

---

[19] Crowe 30. Crowe notes that the Greeks believed that the planets traveled around the earth in an eccentric circle, meaning that the earth was not at the exact center of the orbiting planets, but instead was thought to be a bit off to one side. Thus, the planets would at times be closer to earth, and other times be farther away from it. The Greek term ἀπόγειος literally means "away from earth", and περίγειος means "near the earth".

place opposite to the sun, which also means that, at this point, the planets will be rising at the same time that the sun is setting. When, however, the planets are moving outwards from the point closest to the earth, or their *perigee,* they again come to the place opposite the sun, but at this point, they make their first station and begin to retrace their path, or go retrograde. The planets then move outwards again towards the point of *apogee,* and in doing so, make their second station in opposition to the sun, at which point the whole magnificent transition has occurred, and the planets move on to the next part of their journey.

Section 4
"Nocturnal and Diurnal Planets"
Περὶ ἡμερινῶν καὶ νυκτερινῶν ἀστέρων.

The term *diurnal planets* is used to refer to Saturn and Jupiter, which belong to the same sect as the sun, inasmuch as they do not often make settings or appearances in the night sky. They are most productive during the day and are happiest in diurnal places[20]. Whenever the *nocturnal planets* are mentioned, this refers to Mars and Venus, which have been designated to the sect of the moon. These planets make many appearances, setting often in the evening and thus being seen frequently in the night sky. Mercury, however, shares equally in the two sects. If Mercury is making a morning rising, it falls under the sect of the sun, but if it makes an evening setting, it is in the sect of the Moon.

---

[20] Robbins 43. This seems to be a direct commentary to Book I, Chapter 7 of Ptolemy, but interestingly, Ptolemy and Porphyry give entirely different explanations of why the *nocturnal* and *diurnal* planets have been assigned as such. Ptolemy's explanation focuses on the heat of the day and the moisture of the night. For instance, he suggests that Saturn, which is a cold planet, should be assigned to the day because of its warmth, while Mars is helped by the moisture of the night.

Section 5
"The Naming of Certain Zones and Signs to the Specific Planets"

Περὶ οἴκων οἴτινες καὶ ζῶναι τῶν ἀστέρων προσαγορεύονται.

The circle of the zodiac is divided into twelve sections, which are called the *houses* of the planets, the *zones*, or simply the *zodiacal signs*. The northernmost signs and the ones near to us have been assigned to the lights, the moon ruling the sign of Cancer, and the sun ruling Leo. The next closest signs of Gemini and Virgo have been given to Mercury, while Taurus and Libra are connected with Venus. Mars is said to rule Aries and Scorpio, and Jupiter is the ruler of Sagittarius and Pisces. Lastly, the farthest signs of Capricorn and Aquarius have been given to Saturn.

Section 6 "Exaltation"
Περὶ ὑψωμάτων

The *exaltations* of the stars have been assigned by the subsequent method. For the diurnal planets, the signs that are sympathetic by nature and trine to each planet have been used[21]. In the case of the sun, for example, since it rules the sign of Leo, it will be exalted in the sign of Aries, which is both a four-footed sign and is in a trine relationship to the sign of Leo. The exact degree of exaltation for the sun is 19 degrees of Aries. Since the natural sign of Saturn is Aquarius, Saturn will be exalted at around 20 degrees of Libra. Jupiter, which rules Pisces, will be exalted at 15 Cancer.

Inasmuch as they belong to the sect of the moon, which emits weaker beams than the sun, the nocturnal planets are exalted in the signs sextile to their own signs. For instance, the moon is exalted in the sign sextile to her own sign of Cancer, close to three degrees of Taurus. Mars is exalted in the sign sextile to Scorpio at 28 Capricorn. Venus is exalted at 26 Pisces, which is in the sign sextile to Taurus.

Mercury is exalted in its own sign of Virgo at 15 degrees. This is the case because Mercury is a planet shared between the sects, and also because its rays are more dim on account of it very often making settings. The signs opposite to the exaltations happen to be the *falls* of the planets, or the places in which the planets have the weakest power.

---

[21] Robbins 89-91. In Book I, Chapter 19, Ptolemy also gives an explanation of why the specific exaltations of the planets have been assigned, but his reasons are entirely different from the reasons given by Porphyry. Again, Ptolemy explains the reasons of the exaltations mainly in terms of the planets being hot or cold.

Section 7
"Co-rulers of the Places"
Περὶ συνοικοδεσποτῶν

Two planets are *co-rulers* to each other, whenever one rules a certain sign, and the other is exalted in that sign. Another instance when planets can be called *co-rulers* is when they are *co-ruling* the places or the trigons. Some specific cases are the sun and Mars being co-rulers of Aries, the moon and Venus co-ruling Taurus, Mercury and Saturn co-ruling Gemini[22], Jupiter and the moon ruling Cancer, or Saturn and Venus ruling Libra. Mars, however, is the only ruler of Scorpio. Jupiter and the sun co-rule Sagittarius, Mars and Saturn both rule Capricorn, Saturn and Mercury rule Aquarius, and Pisces is *co-ruled* by Jupiter and Venus.

The king and queen of the heavens are the sun and the moon, also called the "lights" or the "illuminators", the sun ruling during the day, and the moon ruling the night. The sect lights are considered to be co-rulers along with other planets, however, the exaltations of the planets are not considered in this specific case.

---

[22] Saturn is the trigon ruler of Gemini.

Section 8 "Testimony"
Περὶ ἐπιμαρτυρίας

When planets are making angles to one another, it is said that the planets are making a *testimony*. Each of the angles are illustrated hereafter. A trine is created when there are a total of five signs, with the outer two signs being separated by three signs in the middle. The square exists when there are four total signs, not including the two in the middle. An opposition means that there is an aspect coming from two signs that are seven signs apart from one another. The sextile is the angle made from two signs that are three places apart, separated by one sign in the middle[23].

The trine is a sympathetic and helpful aspect, and if a malefic is involved, it will be less damaging than it is in other aspects. The square is a hard, discordant and annoying influence, especially when it includes a malefic. The opposition creates contention and rivalry which becomes worse when involving a malefic. The sextile is a weaker configuration.

It is also essential to observe an aspect, to see whether or not it is a *perfect aspect*, meaning that it is making an angle not only by sign, but also by exact degree. The trine is exactly 120 degrees, the square is 90 degrees, the sextile is 60 degrees, and the opposition is exactly 180 degrees. Often the planets are in aspect to one another by sign, but not by degree.

---

[23] Robbins 73-75. This seems to be connected to Ptolemy Book I, Chapter 13 on "The Aspect of the Signs".

Section 9
"Right-handed and Left-handed Aspects"
Περὶ δεξιῶν καὶ 'ευωνύμων σχεμάτων.

A *right-handed* aspect, including the trine, square, or sextile, occurs when an angle extends backwards out to the sign from which a planet would have departed. It is called a *left-handed* aspect when the aspect is reaching out to the sign to which a planet will travel. For instance, if the sun is in Leo, then the *right-handed* trine of Leo is Aries, while the *left-handed* trine is in Sagittarius. The *right-handed* square of Leo is Taurus, and the *left-handed* square is in Scorpio. The *right-handed* sextile would be Gemini, and the *left-handed* sextile would be Libra. There are seven beams released by each of the planets; three that face upwards or north, three that go downwards or south, and one that shines exactly across to the opposite point. The *right-handed* beams go up, while the *left-handed* beams shine down.

Section 10 "Transmission"
Περὶ παραλλαγῆς

The term *transmission* is utilized whenever a planet passes by the exact degree of an angle, at which point that angle is creating a geometric line that is exactly even on both sides[24]. For example, if the sun is at 19 degrees of Aries, and Saturn advances past the degree of the opposition into 20 degrees of Libra.

---

[24]The Greek here literally says "ἰσοσκελοῦς γραμμῆς", which is unclear in its exact meaning in this short fragment. It means an "equal-sided line" or a line that is "equal on both sides", but this could mean specifically either an opposition (as is described in the example that follows), or an exact aspect in general.

Section 11
"Planets in Union or Closing In on One Another"
Περὶ συναφῆς καὶ κολλήσεως

They call it a *union* and a *closing in* whenever there is a configuration by degree, or there is an aspect that is about to come together within three degrees. It is also termed *closing in* whenever a faster moving planet is approaching a slower moving planet, but the planets are no greater than three degrees apart from one another. Certain authors suggest that, in regards to the moon, these configurations should be considered within a span of thirteen degrees, because the moon travels 13 degrees in the course of one day and one night[25].

Section 12 "Separating"
Περὶ ἀπορροίας

The term *separating* is used whenever a planet is being carried away from the place in which another planet is sitting. Conversely, a "union[26]" refers to a planet that is traveling into another planet or the beam of another planet. For example, suppose the moon is at 20 Scorpio, Saturn is at 10 Scorpio, and Jupiter is at 25 Scorpio. It is clear in this case that the moon is *separating* from Saturn and is moving towards an aspect to Jupiter. And now suppose the moon is at 20 degrees of Scorpio, Saturn is at 10 degrees of Aquarius, and Jupiter is at 25 degrees of Leo. In this case, the moon is separating from the square to Saturn at 10 degrees, at which point Saturn was casting a ray onto the moon. The moon, conversely, is applying to 25 degrees of Scorpio, at which point Jupiter will cast a ray onto the moon from its aforementioned sign of Leo.

---

[25] Robbins 113-117. This section, as well as sections 12 and 13, seem to be directly correlated with Book I, chapter 24 of the *Tetrabiblos*.

[26] For *unions*, see above, section 11.

Section 13
"More on Separating"
Ἄλλως περὶ ἀπορρίας.

The concept of *separating* is also pertinent in the following condition. A planet is said to be *separating* whenever the faster planet is moving away from the slower planet, especially when it has just very nearly applied to make an exact aspect, and is now beginning to have more degrees separating it by aspect than before.

Section 14
"Being Surrounded"
Περὶ περισχέσεως

A planet is said to be *surrounded* whenever it happens to be in the following configuration. For the purpose of example, suppose the moon is in Virgo and Mars is in Aries. Virgo is inherently *surrounded* by the signs of Leo and Libra. Mars casts beams from Aries into the following places; a trine to the sign of Leo and an opposition to the sign of Libra. The moon is thus surrounded by the rays of a malefic. And whenever malefics enclose the moon or the Ascendant, and there are no benefic influences to mitigate these influences, the nativity is said to be short-lived.

Section 15
"Being Enclosed"
Περὶ ἐμπερισχέσεως

The configuration illustrated hereafter also falls under the concept of being *surrounded*, but may more fittingly be called *enclosement*. It is termed *enclosement* whenever two planets surround a planet that sits in the middle, and no other beam of any planet falls into the places between these planets. It is also called *enclosement* when other planets cast a ray into the seven degrees preceding or following a planet, for the planet has just been released from these seven degrees, and is moving into the next seven degrees. This can also apply when the same planet surrounds a planet by different angles, as has been mentioned above. A nativity that has a planet *enclosed* by malefics is very difficult, while a nativity with an *enclosement* by benefics can be quite beneficial.

Section 16 "Intervention"
Περὶ μεσεμβολήσεως

It is labeled *intervening* whenever a planet throws a ray into the degrees between two planets. For instance, if the moon is at 10 Leo and Mars is at 25 Leo, then there are 15 degrees separating these two planets. And if Jupiter happens to be at 12 degrees of Aries, or anywhere between 10 and 25 degrees, then its beam is *intervening* into the space between the moon and Mars. This would also be the case if the moon was at 10 Leo, Jupiter was at 25 Leo, and Mars was in Aries at 12 degrees or anywhere between 10 and 25 degrees. In this case we might say that Mars is *intervening* between the moon and Jupiter.

Section 17
"Transference"
Περὶ μετοχετεύσεως

The term *transference* is relevant whenever a planet comes together with one planet, and then with another planet. When this occurs, the moving planet transfers the power of the first planet onto the power of the second planet.

Section 18
"Collection"
Περὶ ἐπισυναγωγῆς

It is called *collection* whenever two different planets come together with the same third planet. In this instance, the third planet takes on the power of both of the other two planets.

Section 19
"Turning Away"
Περὶ ἀποστροφῆς

The term *turning away* is utilized whenever the Ascendant ruler does not come into an aspect with the ruler of the Ascendant which signifies the things in question[27].

Section 20
"Upon the Tenth"
Περὶ ἐπιδεκατείας

A planet that is sitting in the tenth sign is said to be *upon the tenth* or *superior* from a planet in the fourth. For instance, a planet in Libra is *upon the tenth* in comparison to a planet in Capricorn, while a planet in Capricorn is *superior* to a planet in Aries[28].

---

[27] The Greek here is very vague. The translation here is not definitive.

[28] This passage doesn't quite make sense, since the second example does not exactly follow the explanation of the concept. And beyond that, the grammar in the body of the text doesn't quite fit the sentence. The footnotes, however, do provide an alternate option which does make more sense. I am confident in the translation of the Greek that is written in the critical edition here, but due to the fragmented nature of this section, the true meanings of the terms being described are not entirely clear.

Section 21
"Superiority"
Περὶ καθυπερτερήσεως[29]

In all cases, a planet in the right-hand part of a trine, square, or sextile is said to be *superior* to the planet on the left, for the one on the right is traveling towards the one on the left. For instance, a planet in Capricorn will be *superior* to the planet which it trines in Taurus, the one it squares in Aries, and the one it sextiles in Pisces. Conversely, a planet placed in Libra, Virgo or Scorpio will be *superior* to a planet in Capricorn. They say that a *superior* planet is more powerful, whether by trine or by square. Furthermore, the *superior* planet is always stronger, whether it is a benefic, malefic, or placed in an angular house. If it is a benefic, it is thought to signify a notable chart, but if it is a malefic, is indicates an unremarkable nativity. In general, any star that is on the right is *superior* to a planet on the left, the one to which it is approaching.

---

[29] Robbins 245. The verb καθυπερτερεῖν is used in the *Tetrabiblos*, and there is a footnote that clarifies its meaning. Robbins writes "The anonymous commentator on Ptolemy says that 'stars are said to overcome (καθυπερτερεῖν) when they are of a smaller number of degrees,' i.e. of the zodiac. The right takes precedent over the left, as a general rule."

Section 22
"Juxtaposition"
Περὶ ὁμορήσεως

The term *juxtaposition* is pertinent whenever the planets are in the same bounds, and especially when they are in an applying aspect. This term can also be used when two planets are in an angle to one another from two bounds that are ruled by the same planet.

Section 23
"Void of Course"
Περὶ κενοδρομίας

The phrase *void of course* is used whenever the moon makes no applying configurations, including no conjunctions or any other aspect, either by sign or by degree, within a 30 degree period, nor is it about to make any of the aforementioned aspects. Nativities with this configuration are unremarkable and will bring no advancement.

Section 24
"The Casting of Rays"
Περὶ ἀκτινοβολίας

The leading planet in an aspect *casts a ray* onto the planet behind it. For example, a planet in Aries *casts a ray* by square to a planet in Capricorn, and by trine onto a planet in Sagittarius. Conversely, the planet behind does not *cast a ray* onto the leading planet of an aspect, but instead is said to *look upon* that planet, and because it is approaching that planet, is also said to be *superior*[30] to it, as has been mentioned earlier. For a visual ray of light is carried to the planet in front, while a planetary ray is cast out and carried to the planet in the back.

It is essential to notice whether a planet *casts a ray* only by sign, or also by degree. There are two schools of thought in regard to this concept. Certain authors have said that, when making a square aspect, the planet in the sign to which the planets are traveling will *cast a ray* back onto the planet that is in the sign behind it. For instance, a planet in Cancer *casts a ray* to a planet in Aries, while the planet in Aries *looks upon* the planet in Cancer. If the planet in Cancer is malefic, then it destroys the nature of the one in Aries. The planet that *casts a ray* is destructive, while the planet that merely *looks upon* the other is not[31]. In the case of the opposition, a

---

[30] For one planet's *superiority* to another, see above, section 21.

[31] Robbins 280-281. In his footnotes, Robbins refers to another text and describes the casting of rays as destructive. He suggests that the planetary hurling of a ray might be regarded more like a "missile". He writes, "On projection of rays (ἀκτινοβολία) see Bouche-Leclercq, pp. 247-250. The planets, by their rotation in their orbits moving, as the astrologers said, 'from right to left', 'in the order of the following signs,' 'regard' those that precede them and 'cast rays,' like missiles, at those that follow them; always, however, if the action is to be effective, at the angle of one of the

planet simultaneously *casts a ray* and *looks upon* the planet opposite to its own position. Furthermore, a planet never *casts a ray* by trine, but instead settles its ray upon the closest square aspect, because the trine is a much easier aspect on account of its sympathetic nature. This is one way of comprehending these terms.

Thrasyllus agreed that the *casting of rays* is destructive. But he also said that planets that are *casting rays* from a square or opposition to the Ascendant are destructive, but if these rays are cast into certain degrees that are also being witnessed by trine, they then do not participate in such destruction. Thrasyllus also mentions that the place from which a beam is carried up to the Ascendant degree, but not past the degree of the Ascendant, is the place from which *releasing* shall occur. This also pertains to the degree of the planet which rules the sign of the moon.

More specifically, whenever the planet which rules the sign of the moon is placed in its own sign along with the moon, or is opposite to the moon, then we shall release from the planet ruling the sign of the moon. For instance, if the moon and Jupiter are both in Sagittarius, or the moon is in Sagittarius and Jupiter is in Gemini, then we will release from Jupiter.

---

recognized aspects (opposition, quartile, etc., these two having the greatest offensive force) 280-281."

Section 25 "Chariots"
Περὶ λαμπηνῶν[32]

The planets are considered to be in their *chariots*, whenever they are in their own places, such as their own signs, trigons, exaltations, or bounds. And a planet in this position is quite powerful, even if it is under the beams of the sun. This condition is more strong than others. Furthermore, if the planet is rising or is in an angular house, and can see the moon by aspect, this will be indicative of an authoritative and leadership-oriented nativity. [1. from the left and behind. 2. from the front and the right. 3. from the [ones] on the left. 4....Ptolemy said that this is the same idea as the location from which a ray is carried in a square aspect or an opposition. And Ptolemy also mentioned the trigons of the planets, except that one must look at this concept in regard to co-rulership of places.[33]]

Section 26 "Cooperation"
Περὶ μετοχῆς

It is termed *cooperation* whenever a planet shares the same sign with another planet or looks upon that planet by sign. The planetary co-ruler of a sign is said to be in *cooperation*. And is also co-ruling whenever it is of a place and an exaltation[34].

---

[32] Robbins 111-113. Ptolemy briefly mentions the *chariots* in Book I, section 23.

[33] The fragmented sentences within the brackets here are hard to translate, as they are lacking in context almost altogether. The Latin footnotes note that much of what is written inside these brackets are not the words of Ptolemy, but are instead a reference to Thrasyllus. It is also quite likely that this is actually a comment inserted into the text by a later compiler, such as Demophilus, but that it somehow ended up in the body of the critical edition.

[34] These last two sentences are very fragmented, so the exact meaning is not entirely clear. Thus, the translation here is not definite.

Section 27
"Counteraction"
Περὶ 'ανταναλύσεως

The term *counteraction* is utilized whenever the diurnal planets occupy the signs or exaltations of the nocturnal planets, or the nocturnal planets occupy the signs or exaltations of the diurnal planets. Or, whenever the planets are well-placed and strong in certain signs, but the rulers of the signs in which they fall happen to be poorly situated in unproductive or malefic placements.

Section 28
"Maltreatment"
Περὶ κακώσεως

It is termed *maltreatment* whenever a certain planet is hit by the beams of a malefic, including being enclosed[35] by malefics. A planet is also *maltreated* when it is in a configuration to a malefic or is approaching a malefic, when a malefic is opposing it or superior to it, or if its sign-ruler is a poorly-placed malefic. It is also considered to be *maltreatment* when a planet itself is declining in one of the unproductive places.

---

[35] For planets being *enclosed,* see above, section 15

Section 29
"Keeping Guard"
Περὶ δορυφορίας

There are three ways in which a planet is said to *keep guard*. The first case is when a certain planet, being in its own sign or exaltation and in an angular house, makes an aspect to another planet, which is also in its own sign or exaltation, by casting a ray to the degree preceding that planet.

One illustration of this configuration would be Saturn in Aquarius opposing the sun in Leo. Another example would be Jupiter in Sagittarius trining the sun in Leo. And there are many more examples; Mars in Capricorn opposing Jupiter in Cancer; Jupiter in Sagittarius trining Mars in Aries or opposed to Mercury in Gemini; Mars in Scorpio trine to the moon in Cancer; Mars in Scorpio trine to Jupiter or Venus in Pisces; moon in Taurus being sextile to Jupiter or Venus in Pisces. The moon in Cancer being sextile to Venus in Taurus or trine to Jupiter or Venus in Pisces.

A chart with such a configuration is considered to be great, and if the sect ruler is *keeping guard*, then the nativity is not one of a trivial life, but far from it. Unless, of course, malefics happen to influence everything else in the chart, in which case a strong planet such as this, overseeing everything, will at least be helpful. For no planet which is well-placed in its own sign or exaltation is entirely unproductive.

Another form of *keeping guard* happens when the planets cast rays. For instance, if one of the lights is in the first or tenth houses, but is in a sign other than its own, and a planet of its sect casts a ray onto it, that planet protects the sun or the moon. More specifically, this planet is *keeping guard* when it casts a ray into the degree preceding the sun or conversely, the degree following the moon, into which the moon is approaching; and when she arrives at that degree, the ray will become an equal-sided line. In general, a trine aspect is better at *keeping guard* than a square, opposition, or sextile, all of which are weaker aspects.

The third form of *keeping guard* is as follows. In a diurnal chart, the diurnal planets *keep guard* by being placed upon the Ascendant or the Midheaven. In a night chart, however, the nocturnal planets can *keep guard* by being in the degrees either preceding or following one of these places. The sun might be protected by an aspect thrown from the preceding degree, while the moon will be protected by an aspect being thrown from up to seven degrees past the Ascendant or Midheaven. More specifically, planets that are *keeping guard* and are standing in the 15 degree span rising before the Ascendant or Midheaven cannot harm the sun. And the sun itself also has the power to *keep guard* over planets that are placed along side of it in an angular house, and the moon has a similar power.

The planets can also *keep guard* by sect. The diurnal planets can *keep guard* over the nocturnal planets, or vice versa. But nevertheless, if a planet *keeping guard* is a benefic planet, then the nativity will by no means be unremarkable.

Section 30
"The Sign Ruler, the Lord, and The Ultimate Ruler of the Nativity"
Περὶ 'οικοδεσπότου καὶ κυρίου καὶ 'επικρατήτορος

The *sign ruler* of the nativity, the *lord* of the nativity, and the *ultimate ruler* of the nativity influence each other, and so it is essential to distinguish the subtleties between them. The ancients seemed to have convoluted the terms by not distinguishing clearly one from another. Each of them have their own distinct power, just as the pilot of a ship has a different role than the owner of that same ship. And so we will illustrate here how these terms are intertwined with one another.

The ancient authors have said that the sun is the ruler of the day, and the moon governs the night, and such authors have also made the following distinctions. If the sun is rising in the east in a day chart, then it is chosen as the *ultimate ruler* of the nativity. If, however, the sun is declining in the west, but the moon happens to be in the eastern part of the chart, then the moon is taken as the *ultimate ruler*, and especially if it is rising up to the point of the Ascendant as it makes its passage in to the eastern horizon. If, however, both the sun and the moon are declining in the west, then the Ascendant itself will be the *ultimate ruler*.

In a night chart, the rules are as follows. If the moon is rising in the east, then it is clearly the *ultimate ruler* of the nativity. If, however, it is setting in the west, but the sun is under the horizon of the chart, approaching or near to the Ascendant, then the sun is chosen. In the case that both the sun and the moon are under the horizon, but are in an angular or succedent house, then the moon will be picked as the *ultimate ruler* because it is the ruler of the sect. If, however, the moon is found to be declining in the west, and the sun is in an angular house, then the sun is chosen.

In general, whichever light is closer to the pivots will be assigned as the *ultimate ruler*, then the light that is nearer to the east, and then the light of the sect. If both the sun and the moon are descending, then the Ascendant will be used as the default. And once the *ultimate ruler* of the chart has been found (C), then one can also find the *sign ruler* of the chart, as well as any planets that are *co-rulers* along with that planet.

The ruler of the sign in which the *ultimate ruler* falls will be the *sign ruler* of the chart, and the *co-ruler* will be the planet ruling the bounds in which it is placed. And it is necessary to examine these rulers, to see if they are making a testimony by some kind of aspect to either the Ascendant or the moon. The whole judgment of the nativity will be derived from these things.

Some authors simply take the planetary ruler of the bounds in which the Ascendant falls to be the *sign ruler* of the chart, and they use the ruler of the Ascendant sign as its *co-ruler*. Those same authors use the ruler of the Midheaven as the ruler of the nativity, in the case that it is productive by being in an angular house. If this is not the case, they use any planets that are situated close to the Midheaven, as if such planets are a supreme ruler sitting up high on a throne in the chart, governing all the affairs of the nativity. When it is the case that there are no planets near the Midheaven, they will use any planets that are rising after the Midheaven.

First of all, these authors would use the ruler of the Ascendant or any planets that had walked up and stopped near to the Ascendant, either by sign or by bounds, whether it be the ruler of the moon, or the ruler of the Midheaven, or the ruler of the Lot of Fortune. This planet could be considered as long as it would have been rising or setting within seven days before or after the native's birth, or even would have been making a station within that time (D).

It is of common consent that the planet chosen will be the supreme ruler of the chart, and essentially it controls the nativity. If two planets meet these requirements, then the most powerful planet that is rising will be chosen. The ruler of the sign of the preceding new moon is also taken alongside this ruler. I would suggest also that the ruler of the bounds in which the preceding new moon occurred should also be considered, especially in the case that the moon is separating from the sun. If, however, the moon is waning, then the ruler of the bounds of the full moon should be used.

And from all the planets identified, the planet that is most sympathetic to the nativity should be chosen as the *lord* of the chart, which is the planet that is placed in the most superior position. This would be the planet that is closest to the Ascendant degree or most closely placed in the ascending sign or has the greatest power by being in the closest aspect to the Ascendant.

Next one must examine this *lord* of the nativity by means of the techniques described in the following sections, to see what kind of power it holds. But often times, the process of actually locating the *lord* of the nativity is the most difficult task of all. For at times it is the case that the *lord* of the chart and the *sign ruler* of the chart are the same planet, which occurs whenever the *lord* is found to be the same planet that rules the sign in which the sun or the moon falls, as long as it has been chosen as the light which is the *ultimate ruler* of the whole chart. And in this case, this planet will bring outcomes of great magnitude.

Section 31
"Signs of Correspondence"
Περὶ ὑπακουόντων ζῳδίων[36]

Certain signs are thought to *correspond* to one another, such as Libra and Aries, for whenever the sign of Aries increases the length of the day, the sign of Libra does the opposite by decreasing the length of the day. The same *correspondence* exists between Pisces and Taurus, for when the ascensional time of Taurus is greater, the ascensional time of Pisces is smaller. The other pairs of *corresponding* signs are; Aquarius and Gemini, Capricorn and Cancer, Sagittarius and Leo, and Scorpio and Virgo.

Section 32
"Signs of Equal Power"
Περὶ ἰσοδυναμούντων ζῳδίων

Signs that have the same ascensional times and are also placed in succession to one another are said to be *equal in power*. One example of signs that are *equal in power* are Aries and Pisces, as are Virgo and Libra. In the case where planets are three, four or five signs apart, but have the same ascensional times, these planets are said to only be able to hear one another, as they cannot see each other on account of the shadow created by the earth. Some examples include; Taurus and Aquarius, Gemini and Capricorn, Cancer and Sagittarius, and Leo and Scorpio.

---

[36] Robbins 77. This section seems to be correlated with Book I, Section 15 of the *Tetrabiblos*.

Section 33

"Signs that are Visible to One Another and the Magnitude of the Day"

Περὶ βλεπόντων ζῳδίων καὶ μεγέθους ἡμέρας[37]

It is said that signs are *visible to one another*, when the sun's placement in both signs will bring about the same number of hours of daylight. For this means that both signs create the same *magnitude of the day*. The greatest *magnitude of the day* occurs in zone five when the sun is in Cancer, for when the sun is in this position there will be fifteen hours of daylight during the span of one whole night and day. The day of the least magnitude will occur when the sun is in Capricorn, in which case there will only be nine hours of daylight. The signs of Aries and Libra cut the day equally in half. When the sun is in either Leo or Gemini, there will be fourteen hours of daylight, while Taurus and Virgo will bring thirteen hours. The sun being in Aries or Libra will produce twelve hours of daylight, while Scorpio and Pisces will bring eleven hours, and Aquarius and Sagittarius will produce ten hours. And it is these signs that are said to be *visible to one another*.

---

[37] Robbins 77. This section is also comparable Book I, Section 15 of Ptolemy.

Section 34
"Unconnected Signs"
Περὶ ἀσυνδέτων ζῳδίων[38]

The signs are *unconnected* to one another when they are not similar at all by nature, and especially if they can't see one another by aspect.

Section 35
"Cadent Houses"
Περὶ ἀποκλιμάτων

The term *cadent house* is utilized to refer to the four houses that rise up before the angular houses. Similarly the *succedent houses* are the houses that rise up after the angular houses. With respect to nativities, the portion of the chart extending from the degree of the Ascendant up to the Midheaven is called the eastern region. The southern region reaches from the Midheaven to the Descendant, the western region is taken from the Descendant to the Nadir, and the northern region covers the area from the Nadir to the Ascendant degree.

---

[38] Robbins 77-78. This section seems to be directly correlated to Book I, Section 16 of the *Tetrabiblos*.

Section 36
"Productive Signs"
Περὶ χρηματιζόντων ζῳδίων

According to Timaeus, there are a total of seven *productive* places in a nativity, including the four angular houses, the two houses which are trine to the first house[39], and the house rising up after the tenth house[40]. The remaining houses are unproductive. Often, however, if the greater part of the ascending sign happens to have risen up above the horizon, and thus one of the latter degrees of the sign marks the Ascendant degree, then the sign on the second house will share in the productivity of the first house.

Section 37
"The Conception Sign of the Sun"
Περὶ σπορίμου ζῳδίου Ἡλίου[41]

They call the *conception sign of the sun*, the sign which is in a left-handed square to the sun. For this is the sign that that the sun would have been sitting in ten months earlier, and the sign in which conception would have occurred. While seven months prior, the sun would have been in the sign opposing its current position.

---

[39] the modern equivalent to the fifth and the ninth
[40] the eleventh
[41] Robbins 221-229. Conception charts are mentioned in Book III, Chapter 1 of the *Tetrabiblos*.

Section 38
"The Conception Sign of the Moon"
Περὶ σπορίμου ζῳδίου Σελήνης

Other authors have assigned another technique to the moon. Antiochus suggested that there are two valid methods to consider. In one technique, he examined the moon to see its exact degree, then he added five to this number, and then subtracted this sum from the day of month during which the birth had occurred, up to the number twenty nine, and that was the number of the day during which conception occurred. Antiochus then counted back by use of the astronomical tables to find the sign of the moon during conception.

Petosiris, on the other hand, said that the place in which the moon happened to be during conception, would become the Ascendant sign of the birth chart, or the sign opposite to the Ascendant. And conversely, whatever sign the moon happened to occupy in the birth chart, would be the sign on the Ascendant of the conception chart.

And yet other authors designated the Ascendant of the conception chart as follows. They looked to see which exact degree was on the Ascendant of the birth chart, and they then took the number of degrees that had already risen above the ascending degree and multiplied this number by the number of hours. This sum was then given back to the natal chart, at the rate of thirty degree increments from the Ascending sign, and the place in which this number fell was the Ascendant of the conception chart.

Section 39
" The Twelfth Part"
Περὶ δωδεκατημορίου[42]

The *twelfth-part* of the moon is calculated in two different ways. The first method is calculated hereafter. First, the exact degree of the moon is located. From there, that number of degrees is divided into intervals of two and a half degrees, and the interval in which the degree of the moon falls is assigned as the *twelfth-part* of the moon. For instance, let the moon be at 13 degrees of Aries. I will give the first two and a half degree interval to Aries, the second 2.5 degrees to Taurus, then 2.5 degrees to Gemini, 2.5 degrees to Cancer, and 2.5 degrees to Leo. And thus, the thirteenth degree will fall in the next sign of Virgo, which is ruled by Mercury.

The *twelfth-part* of the sun is calculated by using the exact same method as the moon, as is the *twelfth-part* of the Ascendant. Just as was calculated with the moon, after finding the degree of the Ascendant, the number of degrees that have already risen up can be counted, and this number can be divided into 2.5 degree sections.

Some authors, however, have calculated the twelfth part of the moon differently. These authors have calculated the *twelfth part* as follows. They looked to see how many degrees were between the sun and the moon. Then, they calculated the number of sections of thirty degrees that were within this span between the sun and the moon, and then subtracted out these portions. They then divided the remaining number of degrees into intervals of 2.5, doing so in the sign in which the moon had fallen. If there were less than thirty degrees between the sun and the moon, then we take the

---

[42] Robbins 109-111. The *twelfth part* is mentioned in Book I, section 22 of the *Tetrabiblos*.

number of degrees between the sun and the moon, and that number is divided into 2.5 degree intervals. And it is, of course, necessary to have calculated the boundaries of the Ascendant accurately in accordance with the astronomical tables.

Section 40
"Masculine and Feminine Signs"
Περὶ ἀρρενικῶν καὶ θηλυκῶν ζῳδίων[43]

The *masculine signs*, according to sect, are the signs ruled by the sun, Jupiter, and Saturn. The *masculine signs* begin with Aries and continue around the zodiac with every other sign being masculine. The *feminine signs*, according to the sect of the moon, are the signs belonging to the moon, Venus and Mars. This includes the signs beginning at Taurus, and continuing around the zodiac counting every other sign. From this set of *feminine signs*, however, Capricorn cannot be included and must be disregarded, as it is ruled by the masculine planet of Saturn. The sign of Pisces also cannot be included as it is ruled by Jupiter. Similarly, Aries and Libra must be disregarded from the group of *masculine signs*, as one is ruled by Mars and the other by Venus. Because Mercury is common to both sects, the signs of Gemini and Virgo cannot be considered to be either masculine nor feminine.

---

[43] Robbins 69-71. Book I, Section 12 is correlated to this chapter of Porphyry.

Section 41
"The Ascensional Times of the Signs"
Περὶ τῆς τῶν ζῳδίων ἀναφορᾶς

The zodiacal times are calculated by use of the *ascensional times* of the signs. Each degree of each sign is equivalent to a certain time period. However, all authors have not agreed on these times, and the ancient authors especially seem to have erroneously calculated the *ascensional times*. All of the authors who were living in the region of Alexandria, or in the neighboring cities, calculated the *ascensional times* as follows[44]:

Aries 21° 40'

Taurus 25° 00'

Gemini 28° 20'

Cancer 31° 40'

Leo 35° 00'

Virgo 38° 20'

Libra 38° 20'

Scorpio 35° 00'

Sagittarius 31° 40'

Capricorn 28° 20'

Aquarius 25° 00'

Pisces 21° 40'

---

[44] Robbins 95. Ptolemy comments on this calculation of the ascensional times in Book I, chapter 20.

Ptolemy, who was also near Alexandria, set the *ascensional times* as follows[45]:

Aries 20° 53'

Taurus 24° 12'

Gemini 29° 55'

Cancer 34° 37'

Leo 35° 36'

Virgo 34° 47'

Libra 34° 47'

Scorpio 35° 36'

Sagittarius 34° 37'

Capricorn 29° 55'

Aquarius 24° 12'

Pisces 20° 53'

There would be many errors, in the case that someone who was familiar with the *ascensional times* of the ancients, but did not understand the transmission of these ideas, and might have thought it possible to use the *ascensional times* of the ancients along with Ptolemy's calculations. But again, this would be a mistake. For as a whole, there are two things necessary in order to calculate the "length of life[46]", the first being the distribution of the bounds of the five planets, and the other being the *ascensional times* of the signs.

---

[45] Toomer 101. These ascensional times can be found in the *Almagest* in Book II, section 8.

[46] Robbins 271-307. The section in the *Tetrabiblos* on the "length of life" calculation is quite extensive and shows up in Book III, Section 10.

And there has been much disagreement between the ancient writers and the later authors on the subject of the bounds[47]. In his collection of bounds, Apollinaris disagrees with Ptolemy, and both Apollinaris and Ptolemy differ from Thrasyllus, Petosiris, and the other ancient ambassadors of this knowledge.

As has been mentioned, there has also been disagreement among these authors regarding the *ascensional times* of the signs. The later authors seemed to have had a more thorough understanding of the exact methods needed in order to calculate the *ascensional times* than did the ancients. Nevertheless, the techniques provided by the ancients in regards to their discoveries about the "length of life" seem to have been calculated by using their own collection of *ascensional times*. The ancient authors not only provided broader calculations of the years and the months in relation to the *ascensional times*, but they also divided the years into days and hours. They used their own planetary bounds when calculating the "anaeretic" and the "prorogative" places of a natal chart[48].

It is imperative to not mix together the calculations transmitted from one group with the calculations from the other group. This blending would create an error in regards to Ptolemy's calculation of the "length of life". Instead, one must trace back and use the *ascensional times* and bounds that were corrected and used by Ptolemy, just as one might pursue other ideas which have been noted to be quite useful in terms of understanding these concepts. For Ptolemy has brought this knowledge to us from the teachings of the Chaldeans. And thus we can examine the works of Ptolemy, and try to test out and use his techniques, in order that we might

---

[47] Robbins 91-107. Ptolemy discusses the different calculations of the bounds in Book I, Sections 20 and 21.

[48] Robbins 270-271. The anaeretic (ἀναιρετικός) places are sometimes referred to as the "destructive places". The prorogative (ἀφέτας) places are sometimes translated as "releasing", so this could also be translated as "places of releasing" Robbins notes that the words "aphetic places" are sometimes used, and that the Arabic term for this is the "Hyleg".

obtain similar knowledge and skills. So we will now attempt to lead the way into this knowledge, for the sake of anyone who wants to calculate and discover the "years of life worth living" from a birth chart by use of the *ascensional times*.

The calculation of "the years of life worth living" are derived from the Ascendant degree and the *ascensional times*. For each time period of life is discovered by use of the Ascendant, and in all likelihood, the greatest times of the whole life are derived from the *ascensional times* of the signs. Ptolemy surely did not only use the hourly times, but also from these methods he was able to accurately calculate the divisions in regards to the yearly time periods.

So if it is assumed that each sign, which has 30 degrees, is equal to 30 years, then the total number of years represented by the zodiacal circle is 360 years. This also means that one degree is equal to one year. This proportion has been used in reference to the *ascensional times* of the signs. For instance, in the region of Alexandria, the ascensional time of Aries is 21° 40', which is equal to a time of 21 years and eight months. If this time is then divided by 30 degrees, each degree of the ascending sign becomes equivalent to eight months and twenty days.

Taurus, in the same region and inclination, has an ascensional time of 25° 00', which is equal to 25 years, and when this number is divided by 30, we find that each degree is equal to ten months. If Ptolemy had been in agreement with the ancients when he calculated his ascensional times, he easily would have been able to divide the "great times" into these ascensional times, thus finding the times equivalent to each degree of each sign. But since Ptolemy used different *ascensional times*, or so it seems, it is essential to take them by proportion, in the same way that has been done in the works at hand, by dividing the ascensional times of each sign by thirty degrees.

Section 42

"The Amount of Time Equivalent to Each Degree of Each Ascending Sign"

Ἐν πόσοις χρόνοις ἑκάστη μοῖρα ἀναφέρεται καθ' ἕκαστον ζῴδιον

Each degree that rises is equivalent to a certain amount of time, which is what will be examined here. In most situations, the signs are equal to 30 degrees, however, the ascensional times of each sign are not exactly 30 degrees, but are instead larger or smaller than thirty. For example, the ascensional time of Aries in region one throughout Meroe[49], is 24° 20', which is less than 30 degrees. In this same region, the ascensional time of Taurus is 33° 23', which is greater than 30 degrees[50].

In order to examine the specific amount of time equivalent to each ascending degree, we must first multiply the ascensional time by 60. As an example, we will use the sign of Aries, of which the ascensional time is 24° 20'. By converting this number into minutes, which are its smallest division of sixty, we find that this ascensional time is made up of 1460 minutes. We then divide this number by 30, since this is the standard number of degrees in each sign, and we find that each ascending degree of Aries is equal to approximately 48' 40". Since, in general, each degree can be said to represent one year, we then use this number to calculate the portion of one year represented by each ascending degree, which will be a certain number of months and days. We do this calculation as follows.

---

[49] Toomer 100. The table for this region can be found in the *Almagest*.

[50] Toomer 100. This ascensional time for Taurus is not correct. In Ptolemy's table, Taurus is said to have an ascensional time of 27° 04'. This discrepancy is also mentioned in the Latin footnotes.

As mentioned previously, the ascensional time of Aries in the region of Meroe is 24° 20', which we will multiply by 12, as there are twelve months in each year. Twenty-four degrees times the 12 months represented by each degree gives us a total 288 months. We then look to see how many months are equal to 20 minutes. Since 20 is 1/3 of a total of 60 minutes, it represents one third of a year, which is four months. We then add this number to our previous total of 288 months, bringing the total number of months to 292. Next, we divide this number by 30, to see how many months are represented by each degree. We get an answer of 9 months for each degree, with a remainder of 22 months, which we need to calculate into days by multiplying this number by 30, giving us 660 days. We then divide this number again by 30 degrees, giving us 22 days for each degree, which we then apply to each degree of Aries and Pisces, for they both have the same ascensional times.

Therefore, in the region of Meroe, each of these ascensional degrees represents 9 months and 22 days, which is doubled in the descending degrees, making each descending degree equal to 18 months and 44 days. If this number were tripled, each degree would be equal to two years, five months, and six days. The same method of calculation can be used for each sign in each region (E).

Section 43

"A Method for Distinguishing the Boundaries, by Degree, Between the Angular, Cadent and Succedent Houses"

Πῶς ἔνεστι τὴν διάκρισιν τῶν τε κέντρων καὶ ἐπαναφορῶν καὶ ἀποκλιμάτων μερικῶς διαθέσθαι

In his work on the "length of life", Ptolemy said that one must calculate the "prorogative places" according to a separation of houses that begins with the boundaries of the first house being set up from the five degrees rising up before the ascendant to the 25 degrees rising after the degree of the Ascendant[51]. Ptolemy used this specific 30 degree span as the first house of the chart. This calculation is necessary because, in certain regions, when the point marking the equinox is rising, meaning also that one half of the chart will extend from Aries to Virgo, the eastern quadrant will always be greater than 90 degrees, and the western quadrant will always be less than 90 degrees. In these same regions, the reverse situation will always occur when the "corresponding[52]" sign of Libra is on the Ascendant, making the eastern quadrant less than 90 degrees and the western quadrant greater than 90 degrees.

And in this situation, when dividing the quadrant extending from the Midheaven to the Ascendant into three parts, and assigning the third part to the Ascendant, it is clearly necessary to begin from the degree that has risen up five degrees before the Ascendant degree, and then include the remaining degrees rising up after the Ascendant. After doing this, one can mark the boundaries of the remaining quadrants in the same manner.

---

[51] Robbins, p273. Ptolemy discusses the "length of life" calculation extensively in Book III, Section 10 of the *Tetrabiblos*.

[52] For signs that *correspond* to one another, see above, Section 31

If, however, someone were to suggest that it is more fitting to take this calculation by using the six degrees that have risen above the Ascendant degree, then he would not be thinking clearly. For if it were the case that the area between the Midheaven and the Ascendant were 72 degrees, then the next quadrant would clearly have to be 108 degrees. In this case, the three houses in the eastern quadrant would each equal 24 degrees, and the three houses in the western quadrant would each equal 36 degrees. So if the division were to start at 4 degrees before the Midheaven degree, and were to take the 20 degrees after it as the first division in the quadrant, and the eleventh and twelfth houses would add up to 48, then this would leave only 4 degrees prior to the Ascendant degree. For if the total quadrant is 72 degrees, and 68 degrees are subtracted, this leaves 4, which will mark the degree of the Ascendant.

It is necessary, however, from this method to have six degrees before the Ascendant, because one sixth of 36 is six. And so this method is impossible. But it is also impossible to allot 30 degrees to each house by use of the ascensional times. In five or six regions, if we included six ascensional degrees of Pisces and extended this up to the Midheaven, there would scarcely be 60 degrees[53]. And in this case we would have nothing to provide to the third house in this quadrant, as there would not be enough degrees, which is why it is also not possible to allot 30 degrees to each house. Another example of this would be if we had Aquarius rising and Sagittarius on the Midheaven, which would give us a quadrant equal to 70 degrees. This is also not large enough to give 30 degrees to each house. These examples highlight the reason why it is necessary to mark the houses beginning with the five degrees that rise up prior to the Ascendant, and to then portion out the remaining houses accordingly.

---

[53] Toomer 102-103. See the tables of ascensional times in the *Almagest*.

Section 44
"The Parts of the Body Signified by Each Sign"
Περὶ τοῦ ποῖον μέλος τοῦ σώματος ἕκαστον τῶν ζῳδίων κεκλήρωται

Each of the signs signify certain parts of the body, which are necessary to know, whenever one might foresee an injury. Aries rules the head, Taurus rules the tendons and the throat, Gemini rules the shoulders and the arms, Cancer governs the chest and the ribs, and Leo rules the diaphragm, stomach and the belly. Virgo is associated with the abdomen and the flanks, Libra rules the kidneys and the buttocks, Scorpio rules the genitals and the secret and fruitful places, Sagittarius governs the knees, along with the groin, and the bending of the elbows. Capricorn rules the lower back and the hips, Aquarius is associated with the calves and the ankles, and Pisces rules the feet.

Section 45
"The Parts of the Body Ruled by Each of the Planets"
Ποίων ἕκαστος τῶν ἀστέρων κυριεύει μερῶν[54]

They suggest that the planets signify the following things within the human body. Saturn rules inflammation and dampness, the trachea, and the releasing of the bowels. Jupiter is associated with the liver, and more specifically, the condition of the liver, as well as the tendons beneath the stomach. Mars is said to rule the blood, the kidneys, and the sperm ducts. Venus rules the lungs and the bile. Mercury is connected to the sense of hearing, the windpipe, and the tongue. The sun rules the heart, and the place of life and breath, which is responsible for perceptible movement or perception by the senses. It also governs the sense of sight, and especially the right eye in men and the left eye in women. The moon rules the body as a whole, and more specifically, it rules the spleen, the membranes and the marrow. It also rules the left eye in men and the right eye in women.

In general, Saturn rules long-lasting affairs and chronic conditions. It is also connected with coldness and moisture and with ancient works that have been stored up over time, with foundations and the earth. It represents things that are old, elders, people who are infertile and childless, sailors, completion, extreme wickedness lurking within, slander, envy, ill-will, trouble, terrible things, prison, hair growth and brutality, all gloomy things in life, and clever kinds of torture. When Saturn is configured well in the natal chart, and is productive because of being in one of its own places or chariots, it is helps the native by increasing harm that happens to other people. When, however, Saturn is configured poorly by aspect, it

---

[54] Robbins 317-333. Correlates to Book III, Chapter 12.

brings upon hardships to the native himself. Saturn is also called Φαίνων, or "The Shiner".

Jupiter indicates magnificence, honor, dignity, enjoyment, and a good nature. It also indicates leadership and a good reputation, children, and a person who guides large crowds of people and is received well by them. Jupiter is also called Φαέθων, which means "To Shine".

The fiery planet of Mars is blood-red in color, much like blood that has been heated up and brought to the surface by means of a branding iron. It is also responsible for the traveling of sperm that creates a fetus inside of a women, and is connected to the energy and movement of the soul and the natural impulses, courage, the life force, deceitful affairs, and suffering at the hands of a sour man. Mars also rules military affairs, wars, and the using of iron. It is connected with all kinds of trauma that occur on account of swiftness or mental disturbance. Mars is also called Πυρόεις, or the "Fiery-One".

The sun rules the life breath and the perception of the soul existing within each of us, as well as the movement of the soul itself. It also rules paternity and the characteristic of leadership. And because Venus travels very near to the sun, it receives its brilliance and luster from the rays of the sun. If Venus were to be situated too close to the sun, she would appear to be covered in soot, on account of being burned by the rays of the sun. But because she is far enough out of range, she appears quite beautiful and brilliant. Thus, Venus represents cheerfulness, physical beauty, symmetry, purity, the brilliance of life, good manners, royalty, and priesthood. She is also connected to the wearing of gold, and all things dainty and feminine. Also, because Venus is placed so closely to the sun, which is the soul-giving planet of the cosmos, and she takes on the sun's characteristics by being under its beams, Venus is also said to bring tenderness, affection, love, yearning, marriage, religion, craftsmanship[55], musical ability, and theatrical ability. She is related to all things feminine, the mother, and the siblings. They call her Φωσφόρος, or the "Morning-Star".

When Mercury is approaching the sun, it appears to be throbbing, and Mercury can rarely be seen in the sky as it is quite often situated right under the beams of the sun. And because it rises and sets under the light of the sun, Mercury is influenced by the sun's authority, and thus also rules the movement of the soul. Mercury, in specific, rules the purpose and intentions of the mind, and all things connected with the mind; education, commerce, daily interactions, friendship, fellowship, contracts, brotherhood, service, and all the characteristics of young people, children, and babies. They call him Στίλβων, or the "Glistening-One".

The moon, traveling around the earth, dispenses her greatness onto the planets, and also receives energy from the planets as she passes over them. By virtue of her influence, the moon is connected to the health of the body, including all of the individual parts of the body. She also rules the health of the mother and the health of the queen.

---

[55] The body of the text shows the Greek phrase τῶν κοσμικῶν ἀρχῶν, which doesn't make much sense in the context of this section. The footnotes show an alternate option of τεχνῶν, which makes more sense, so I have translated the body of the text according to the alternate option.

Section 46
"The Clothing, Dyes and Colors Ruled by Each Planet"
Περὶ ὧν ἱματισμῶν καὶ βαφῆς κυριεύουσιν ἢ χροιᾶς

Saturn rules dye that is like castor. Jupiter rules the light white color of milk that is decreasing[56]. Mars, the fiery planet, is associated with the color of flames. The sun rules a pale, golden hue, and Venus rules white skin. Mercury is associated with a dark blue color. And the moon is likened to the color of light green, like the color of a leek.

Section 47
"The Thirty-Six Decans and The Paranatellonta and Their Associated Characteristics"
Περὶ τῶν λς΄ δεκανῶν καὶ τῶν παρανατελλόντων αὐτοῖς καὶ προσώπων

The circle of the zodiac is divided into twelve parts, which are designated as the twelve zodiacal signs. The ancient authors also proposed a method of dividing the circle into thirty-six sections, which they called the *decans*. Because these sections are created by dividing each sign into three sections, each of them being exactly ten degrees, they chose the term *decan*[57]. The stars that rise up alongside the *decans* are called the *paranatellonta*, and they have similar characteristics to the seven planets, for the planets have certain sympathies to the stars being situated upon them.

---

[56] The Greek here is a bit vague, and thus the translation is a bit coarse.

[57] the Greek word for ten is "deka"

For instance, if the sun is placed at 10 degrees of Aries, it is then situated in the first *decan* of Aries, and it will take on the characteristics of Mars. We have mentioned previously that the sun signifies the soul, and so we find that the sun in this placement represents a soul that is manly, passionate, combative, loving of weapons, etc. Conversely, if the sun is placed in the second *decan* of Aries, at 20 degrees, it will take on the characteristics of the sun. The soul will thus be brilliant, honorable, and ambitious, but it will not be combative. Suppose the sun were at 30 Aries, in the third *decan* of the sign of Aries. It would then assume the characteristics associated with Venus, and the native would have a feminine soul with a feminine figure, but also be homely and lustful.

The characteristics associated with the different *decans* have somehow been described only in relation to the soul. These significations, along with the description of the *paranatellonta* and their related characteristics, have been laid out by Teucer of Babylon.

Section 48
"The Fixed Stars and the Power of the Paranatellonta"
Περὶ τῶν ἀπλανῶν λαμπρῶν ἀστερων καὶ τῶν παρανατελλόντων δυνάμεων

The characteristics of the zodiacal signs, and their *paranatellonta*, have been developed by using a synthesis of all the stars involved[58]. Among the fixed stars, there are different levels of brilliance; there are stars that are quite bright, stars that are more dim, and stars that are very dismal. Having taken up a study of these stars, the ancient authors have suggested that the most brilliant stars are also the greatest in magnitude, while the more dim stars are second greatest in power. These authors assigned such levels of power to the fixed stars, continuing on to a sixth level of stars with the weakest magnitude, which they assigned to the most faint stars.

Some of these stars happen to fall within the circle of the zodiac, some being in the northern half, and some being in the southern half. And having examined these stars, the ancient authors found a total of 30 fixed stars in the zodiacal circle that could be placed into the first or second level of magnitude, some of them being very very bright, and others being very brilliant but not as bright as the first group. These authors found that, whenever one of these stars is situated on the Ascendant or the Midheaven, or is making an aspect to the sun or the moon or any other planet, it alters the nativity by blending its energy with the planet or point to which it is near. For example, if the star is blending with a benefic, the luck of the native will increase, but if it is blending energies with a malefic, the native's luck will be less forthcoming.

---

[58] Robbins 47-59. Ptolemy describes the characteristics of the fixed stars in Book I, Section 9.

Section 49

"The Bounds According to the Egyptians, and Ptolemy and the Dark Degrees"

Περὶ τῶν ὁρίων κατ' Ἀιγυπτίους καὶ Πτολεμαῖον καὶ λαμπρῶν καὶ σκιαρῶν μοιρῶν

The ancient authors also divided the signs into smaller parts, which they called the *bounds*. In order to calculate the *bounds*, they did not divide the signs into equal sections, as they did with the decans, but instead divided them up according to another method of reasoning, which has been described in relation to the *final periods* of the planets. I have mentioned the *final periods* of the planets in some previous sections. The same degrees of the *bounds* are laid out by each sign. Certain sections of the *bounds* are related to Jupiter, some are connected with Venus, some to Saturn, and this applies to the remaining planets as well.

Whenever one of the planets is found to be in the sign of a benefic and also in the *bounds* of a benefic, it is said to have a good affect on the nativity, as it magnifies the fortune of the native. If, however, a planet is found to be in the sign of a benefic, but it is in the bounds of a malefic, then the good fortune is weakened. If, on the other hand, a planet is situated in both the sign and the bounds of malefics, then the luck is ruined.

For the energy of the *bounds* might alter the outcomes that are written in the stars, just as they say that the decans take on the characteristics of the planets and stars involved. Ptolemy did not agree with some of the *bounds* laid out by the Egyptians[59]. And so I feel compelled to mention the following things. The previous authors included their discussion of the *bounds* only in regards to the

---

[59] Robbins 91-97. Ptolemy describes the Egyptian calculation of the bounds in Book I, Section 20.

54

possible significations of the *bounds*. They did not make much mention of the different levels of brilliance among degrees, such as the brilliant degrees, dark degrees, and the dim degrees. Unless, however, the planets were found to fall in the most brilliant degrees. And so I have illustrated these concepts in the sections prior to this one.

Section 50
"The Assigning of the Parts of the Body to the Signs"
Περὶ τῆς τῶν ζῳδίων μελοθεσίας[60]

He has made an arrangement regarding the parts of the human body, of which limbs and parts each of the signs and planets rule. Through this knowledge, we might know of possible accidents or injuries, which are gleaned from the Lot of Fortune, the Lot of Daemon, the Lot of Injury, and their rulers. Most often these indications point out pain and suffering, but by having proclaimed everything correctly beforehand, one has certainly released himself from such things. And I have arranged them by the energetic power of their configurations.

---

[60] In their introduction to the text, Boer and Weinstock suggest that section 50 is a paraphrase of Chapter 44, written by an excerptor.

Section 51

"An Outline of the Different Methods for Calculating Trines, Squares, Sextiles, and Oppositions"

Περὶ τριγώνων καὶ τετραγώνων καὶ ἑξαγώνων καὶ διαμέτρων καὶ τῶν ἀσυνδέτων λόγον ἐχόντων πρὸς ἄλληλα ὡς ἐν τύπῳ διαμέτρων

There have been different uses of the trine, sextile, and square configurations. The first of these methods, and the greatest of all, is the method that examines these configurations by degree, as can be seen in the works of Ptolemy, which have been outlined in the earlier sections. The second use of the aspects concerns time, and certain authors including Antigone and Phnaes of Egypt, have called this method the "isosceles triangle of the ascensional times of the signs." The third method is connected with the common and general signs, into which we all might wander[61].

Perhaps the sun is around 1 Leo and Jupiter appears at 5 Sagittarius, which makes a trine from Jupiter to the sun, meaning of course that these shining planets are in aspect to one another. They are not, however, arranged within 120 degrees of one another by width, nor by general time, nor ascensional time (F).

He has called it a sign-based configuration, when a certain planet has the energy of an aspect, either a trine, square or sextile, but the two planets are not connected by degree, nor by time. In the previous sections, we have discussed degree-based aspects, according to the rules set up by Ptolemy, and now we will explain

---

[61] This line seems a bit out of context, but according to the Greek that is written, this is what it must mean. The verb is conjugated in the first person plural form, and thus must mean "we wander".

the sign-based aspects, but in doing so, it seems necessary to use an example based on the ascensional times.

Let the sun be at 1 Aries in the region of Alexandria, let Jupiter be at 12[62] Leo, and let Mars be at 5 Leo. And then we will do the following. The ascensional time of Aries is 21° 40', the ascensional time of Taurus is 25° 00', Gemini is 28° 20' and Cancer is 31° 40'[63]. Thus, the total of these ascensional times is 106° 40', and when this number is subtracted from 120°, we get a remainder of 13° 20', which I have found to be equivalent to about 11.5° Leo. This number of 11.5° Leo has been derived by first multiplying the ascensional time of Leo, which is 35°, by 2, from which we get 70 degrees. We then multiply 70 by 11.5 and we get 805, which is then divided by 60°, giving us 13° 25'. I have added this number to the 106° 40', giving us a total of 120° 05'. This calculation shows that, in the region of Alexandria, the degree of 11.5 Leo will make the first side of an isosceles triangle, as it connects to 1° Aries.

From this calculation, we can conclude the following. Jupiter, in this configuration, makes both a sign-based and time-based trine to the sun, but Mars only makes a sign-based trine to the sun.

Now let us continue with our previous calculations. Since the remainder of the ascensional time of Leo is 21° 35'[64], I have calculated the second side of the isosceles triangle as follows. First I will add 21° 35' to the ascensional time of Virgo and Libra, which are both 38° 20', giving us a total of 98° 15'. If we subtract this

---

[62] In the body of the text, this is written as the number is "2", which doesn't make mathematical sense. The number 12 is in the footnotes and does make sense, so I am using it here.

[63] For the table of ascensional times provided by Porphyry, see above, Section 41.

[64] The remainder of the ascensional time of Leo should be more than this number, a discrepancy which shows up later when Porphyry refers to the remainder of Scorpio as well. The two seeming "errors" add up to almost five degrees, which are mentioned at the end of the section.

from 120°, we get 21° 45', which I have found to be equivalent to around 18.7° of Scorpio. For if we double the ascensional time of Scorpio, which is 35°, we get 70°, and when we multiply this by 18.7°, we get 1305°[65]. I will then divide this number by 60°, giving us 21° 45', and then I add this to 98° 15', from which we get a total time of 120°. Therefore, in the region of Alexandria, the second side of an isosceles triangle would extend from 11.5° Leo to 18.7° Scorpio.

Since this leaves a remainder of 13° 15'[66] of Scorpio, we must add this to the ascensional times of the next signs, and by doing so, we can calculate the third leg of this isosceles triangle. So we will now add up the following ascensional times; Scorpio 13° 15', Sagittarius 31° 40', Capricorn 28° 20', Aquarius 25° 00' and Pisces 21° 40'. The total of these ascensional times will be 119° 55'. And the calculation described above illustrates the method for calculating three equal sides throughout the circle of the zodiac. The five extra degrees have been set aside for special use in regards to the first side of the triangle representing the regular time of 120 degrees. This same time-based method can also be used to find the equal sides of a square or sextile configuration.

---

[65] This number should actually be a bit lower, it seems that the author has rounded up to 18.7 from 18.64.

[66] Again, this is a bit low, but is explained at the end of the section.

Section 52

"The Times of Life in Regards to the Angular, Cadent and Succedent Houses"

Περὶ τῶν χρόνων τῶν κέντρων καὶ ἐπαναφορῶν καὶ ἀποκλιμάτων

The first house indicates the first period of the life, the tenth house indicates the middle age of the life, and the seventh house represents the end of the life. The fourth house then represents the death, as well as the fate of the native after death, as in whether or not the native will happen upon glory and honor or disgrace.

The house that rises up before the first house signifies the labor pains of birth, and the experience of the mother during the gestational period of the native. The first house, then, represents the end of the gestational period, which is marked by the native's birth, as well as the time period directly after birth. The house that ascends after the first house signifies the latter period of the beginning of the life.

The house that ascends before the Midheaven indicates the first parts of the middle age of the life, while the tenth house itself represents the middle part of the middle period of life. And thus the house that rises after the tenth house indicates the latter part of the middle years.

The house that rises before the descendant signifies the first period of the end of the life, while the seventh house itself represents the middle period of the end of the life, and the house that rises after the seventh house symbolizes the last part of the end of life.

The house that ascends before the house opposite to the tenth connotes the time period just prior to death. The fourth house itself shows the native's actual death, while the house that rises after the fourth house indicates the time directly after death.

Each of the houses is calculated by taking the 5 degrees rising up before it and the 25 degrees rising up after it, but only in the case that the quadrants are exactly 90 degrees. If the four quadrants are not exactly 90 degrees, then the degrees of the quadrants must instead be divided into three equal sections. And from this division one is able to calculate how many degrees of each sign would fall into each house.

For example, if the Midheaven is exactly 96 degrees from the Ascendant, and the Descendant is 84 degrees from the Midheaven, then the next two quadrants would follow this pattern accordingly. The quadrant extending from the Nadir to the Descendant would also be 96 degrees and the area from the Ascendant to the Nadir would be 84 degrees. Using this information, the houses can be systematically laid out by dividing these quadrants into three equal sections, starting from the point that rises five degrees above the exact ascendant degree. It is by using this aforementioned process that the twelve house divisions can be derived[67].

---

[67] This is a perfect description of the modern "Porphyry" house system.

Section 53
"The Manners Through Which the Indications of the Planets Come to Fruition"
Ἐκ πόσων τρόπων γίνεται τὰ ἀποτελέσματα τῶν πλανητῶν

There are eleven indications in a nativity that confirm whether or not the proposed outcomes of the planets will actually come to pass. The first indication is when a planet is situated in a good place from the Ascendant, being either in one of the angular houses, or in a house that cooperates with the angles, meaning a house that can be seen by the Ascendant.

The second indication that a planet will bring about what is promised is whenever it is in one of its own places, including its own sign, trigon, exaltation, bounds, or face. A planet is also very strong when it is in a place in which it rejoices.

The third situation indicating a strong planet is when it is not moving retrograde in the natal chart, but is instead moving forward.

The fourth indication is when a planet is not conjunct to a malefic planet, nor is it squared or opposed by a malefic.

The fifth thing to notice is that a planet will not be very strong when it is in a place from which it cannot see the Ascendant. It will also be unproductive when it is in its fall.

The sixth indication of a productive planet is when a benefic[68] planet is receiving it.

---

[68] The word ἀγαθοποιός is not in the body of the text, but it is suggested as a possible correction in the footnotes. Without this word in the

The seventh placement that is likely to bring events to fruition occurs when the planets that are further out from the sun, which are also the masculine planets, meaning either Saturn, Jupiter or Mars, are rising near to the Ascendant. A planet in this position is especially strong if it rises early in the day. It is also a very powerful configuration when the feminine planets, or the planets closer to the sun, are setting near the Descendant. It is an even stronger configuration when Venus, Mercury or the moon are setting in the evening.

The eighth situation occurs when a planet is sitting in its own "light", meaning that the masculine planets are above the hemisphere during the day, but are below it during the night, and the same is true of the feminine planets.[69]

Ninth, the planets tend to manifest their proposed outcomes when they are in fixed signs.

Tenth, a planet is strong when it is in the "heart" of the sun, and especially when it is upon the degree of the sun (G). The benefics in this placement will strengthen a good indication, while the malefics here will amplify a bad indication.

And the eleventh and last indication that a planet will bring about its proposed outcomes occurs when the masculine planets fall in the masculine quadrants, or the feminine planets fall in the feminine quadrants. This also applies when the masculine planets are situated in masculine signs and the feminine planets are sitting in feminine signs.

---

sentence, it would translate as "...when a planet is receiving it". I have included "benefic" in the text, as it seems much more correct in meaning, although it is not a definitive translation of the sentence.

[69] The Greek construction here seems like the writer meant to say that the feminine planets are the opposite in this case. Although this seems like an error in the Greek itself, I am translating this true to what the Greek says, and not compensating for this possible mistake.

Section 54

"A Consideration Regarding the Testimony of the Planets"

Ἔκθεσις εἰς τὰς μαρτυρίας τῶν πλανητῶν

The subject of the *testimony* of the planets is included here, so that there is no ambiguity as to whether or not the proposed indications of a specific planet will be fulfilled. For whenever a planet is in its own place, meaning its own sign, trigon, exaltation, bounds, or decan, then if something is signified by that planet, it will indeed come to pass. There are, however, also four other ways in which the planets *rejoice*, thus strengthening their ability to make things happen.

The first manner in which the planets *rejoice* is by being in certain houses, and these placements are as follows; Mercury in the first house, the moon in the third house, Mars in the sixth, the sun in the ninth, Jupiter in the eleventh, and Saturn in the twelfth house.

The second means by which the planets *rejoice* is by being placed in certain signs. Saturn rejoices in Aquarius, Jupiter in Sagittarius, Mars in Scorpio, the sun in Leo, Venus in Taurus, Mercury in Virgo, and the moon in Cancer.

The third placement of *rejoicing* occurs when the masculine planets are rising near the Ascendant, or the feminine planets are setting near the Descendant.

The fourth condition of *rejoicing* occurs when the masculine planets are placed in the masculine quadrants and the feminine planets fall in the feminine quadrants.

Mercury *rejoices* along with both, that is to say, whenever it is together with the masculine planets, it rejoices with them, and whenever it is with the feminine planets, it rejoices in their placements.

Section 55
"The Beams of the Planets"
Περὶ τῶν ἀκτίνων τῶν πλανητῶν

Each beam from the sun reaches a total span of thirty degrees, extending out 15 degrees in front and 15 degrees behind the beam. A moon beam covers an area of 24 degrees total, reaching out 12 degrees on either side. A beam from Saturn or Jupiter extends to a span of 18 degrees, affecting 9 degrees each way, while Mars covers 16 degrees total, 8 degrees on either side. Lastly, Venus and Mercury have beams that reach a total of 14 degrees, extending out 7 degrees in both directions.

APPENDIX

Appendix of Scholia by Demophilus (or Theophilus)

Section 2

(A) There is a table in Greek in the footnotes here, and the Latin commentary mentions that this table was included in the text, and was found in the lower margin of most of the codices. The table is as follows:

Sun	Spring	Summer	Fall	Winter
Moon	half-moon	full moon	half-moon	concealment
	moist	hot	dry	cold

(B) There is a paragraph of commentary in Greek at the bottom of the page here. The Latin notes mention that this paragraph forms the end of Section Three in all books that they utilized. The footnote, however, is actually placed in Section Two and seems to better apply to Section Two, and thus I have noted it here. The whole note, however, is very vague grammatically, especially since there is very little context from which to extract the true meaning. And thus, this translation is not, by any means, definitive. The Greek is as follows:

The fifteen degrees rising up before and next to it. It must be understood that it is not the exact degree rising up before or after the the sun, but in accordance with what follows, the fifteen degrees [before or after]. For when Venus is preceding the sun, she has the power to appear in the evening and when she is following the sun she appears in the morning. A philosopher says that when a planet is moving forward, that planet will make a movement in the degrees following the sun, but when a planet is retracing its path, there will be movement in the degrees preceding the sun as the planet is changing position. For retrograde motion is subtractive in length, and thus it is called the "leading planet".

Section 30

(C) There is a footnote written in Greek here, and as Boer and Weinstock note in their introduction, it is uncertain as to whether the commentator was Demophilus or Theophilus. The Greek translates as follows:

Scholion from Demophilus/Theophilus. Having chosen the *ultimate ruler*, he examines the destructive rays of the malefics by square and by opposition and by sextile up until ninety and also the ascensional times in order to see what kind of harm might come to the life. For a benefic casting a ray into the degrees following a destructive degree up until five degrees or greater will have power, or if it is in the same bounds this maltreatment might be counteracted.

(D) There is a footnote written in Greek here, also by Demophilus (or Theophilus), that says:

It is necessary to note not only the phase that is rising, but it is also necessary to take the phase that is setting, and also the station. And Dorotheus suggested that the setting phases and the traversing of the stars must also be considered.

Section 42

(E) There is a footnote in Greek here, and as Emilie Boer mentions in her introduction to the text, this note may be evidence that there are parts of Porphyry that are missing from the text. Her reasoning is that the author of this note mentions a possible section in existence about the "length of life". The Greek translates as follows:

Scholium. He explained thoroughly the manner in which it is necessary to divide up the ascensional times and the hourly times. And from these [divisions] they examine the years. In each region, the hourly times are laid out by each sign and each degree, of which they deemed it fit to determine the years and the months by changing them. Whenever the chart was diurnal, they determined the aforementioned hourly times by planet, and in a nocturnal chart, by the times in opposition to these times. The contents of this note will become clear in the [section] on the length of life.

Section 51

(F) There is a note in Greek that is inserted into the text here. The Latin footnotes mention that it was a note written by the excerptor. It translates as follows:

The remainder comes from the summation of the planets.

Section 53

(G) There is a footnote here comparing some Greek passages. They are as follows:

Cf. *Catal.*, I, p. 145, 26 Stars that are in the heart [of the sun] are said to be traveling together with the sun by degree, either near to the degree or on the degree.

Nonn., XXXVIII, 391 ...and having the same course and traveling at the same degree, the ones who have knowledge of the stars have called this [being in] the heart of the sun.

Works Cited

Crowe, Michael J. Theories of the World: From Antiquity to the Copernican Revolution. Mineola: Dover Publications, 2001.

Emilsson, Eyjólfur, "Porphyry", The Stanford Encyclopedia of Philosophy (Fall 2009 Edition), Edward N. Zalta (ed.), URL = <http://plato.stanford.edu/archives/fall2009/entries/porphyry/>.

Gingerich, Owen. The Eye of Heaven: Ptolemy, Copernicus, Kepler. New York: The American Institute of Physics, 1993.

Holden, James Herschel. A History of Horoscopic Astrology. Tempe: American Federation of Astrologers, Inc., 1996.

Plotinus. Plotinus II. Trans. A. H. Armstrong. Cambrideg: Harvard University Press, 1966.

Ptolemy, Claudius. Almagest. Trans. G. J. Toomer. New Jersey: Princeton University Press, 1998.

Ptolemy, Claudius. Tetrabiblos. Trans. F. E. Robbins. Cambridge: Harvard University Press, 1940. Print.

Smith, Mark A. "Ptolemy's Theory of Visual Perception: An English Translation of the "Optics" with Introduction and Commentary." Transactions of the American Philosophical Society: Volume 86, Part 2. Philadelphia: The American Philosophical Society, 1996.

Whitfield, Peter. Astrology: A History. New York: Harry N. Abrams, Inc, 2001.

www.ingramcontent.com/pod-product-compliance
Lightning Source LLC
Chambersburg PA
CBHW071742090426
42738CB00011B/2538